Discover the Power of Goodness and Find Your Answers

Keith Trumbo

World rights reserved. This book or any portion thereof may not be copied or reproduced in any form or manner whatever, except as provided by law, without the written permission of the publisher, except by a reviewer who may quote brief passages in a review.

The author assumes full responsibility for the accuracy of all facts and quotations as cited in this book. The opinions expressed in this book are the author's personal views and interpretations, and do not necessarily reflect those of the publisher.

This book is provided with the understanding that the publisher is not engaged in giving spiritual, legal, medical, or other professional advice. If authoritative advice is needed, the reader should seek the counsel of a competent professional.

Copyright © 2021 Keith Trumbo
Copyright © 2021 TEACH Services, Inc.
ISBN-13: 978-1-4796-1414-1 (Paperback)
ISBN-13: 978-1-4796-1415-8 (ePub)
Library of Congress Control Number: 2021919254

All scripture quotations, unless otherwise indicated, are taken from *The Holy Bible*, *New International Version*®, NIV® Copyright © 1973, 1978, 1984, 2011 by Biblica, Inc.™ Used by permission. All rights reserved worldwide.

Scripture quotations marked NKJV are taken from the NEW KING JAMES VERSION®. Copyright ©1982 by Thomas Nelson, Inc. Used by permission. All rights reserved.

For more books, materials, videos, and information, go to KeithTrumboBooks.com

Dedication

I would like to dedicate this book to all those who seek to understand that truth without love is not truth and love without truth is not love.

Table of Contents

Chapter One: Paralyzed Love 9

Chapter Two: A New Beginning 15

Chapter Three: Seeking Goodness 22

Chapter Four: Faith 29

Chapter Five: The Problem 36

Chapter Six: An Example 41

Chapter Seven: Goodness 48

Chapter Eight: More About Understanding
　　　　　　　His Goodness 57

Chapter Nine: Embracing Goodness 66

Chapter Ten: Doing the Right Thing 73

Chapter Eleven: Getting Answers 81

Chapter Twelve: Answers from His Word 90

Review: Discover the Power of Goodness and Find
Your Answers　　　.. 98

Preface

This simple reality exists: the life you live today reflects the answers you have believed in the past—answers to the deepest questions in your soul. Take a moment and consider some of the big decisions you have made in life. The answers you received to the most important questions in your heart provided direction in making those decisions.

If you are happy with the answers you have and the choices you have made—and are making—in life, this book is not for you. If you have a hunger to discover something vital about how you answer the most important questions you have in life—answers that will inform the decisions you make—then this book is for you.

You can discover how to receive real help from Someone who always has your best interests in mind when it comes to making decisions. You can receive real help from Someone Who delights in seeing you succeed and has made a complete commitment to helping you embrace the best options in life.

This book was written to help you get real answers from the Someone.

CHAPTER ONE

Paralyzed Love

Before I share with you how to get answers to your deepest questions, I feel it is important to share my own story and background. Before I reached the age of twenty-seven, I never went to church; I cruised down the road of life with the accelerator all the way to the floor—that's the way I lived. I had a big chocolate donut in one hand and a giant-sized cup of coffee in the other, as I steered with my knees, as happy as I could be. As a proud American male, I didn't even think about stopping to ask for directions. I had my eye on the prize, determined to finish in first place with no one slowing me down. I lived my life my way.

However, as you can imagine with this winner-take-all perspective, when I reached twenty-seven years of age, my life had not worked out the way I planned. So I went searching for answers. I started asking myself some serious questions.

My search for answers began with an invitation from a friend named Robert. Robert had a calm, noble spirit and was always ready to tell me how he had become a born-again Christian. One day he asked me if I would like to meet with a person whom he called a "channeler." He described how she had helped him understand more about the life he could live. With an open mind and a searching heart, I accepted the invitation.

The channeler—we'll call her Sylvia—lived in a conservative, middle-class neighborhood. I would describe her as a well-educated, down-to-earth person. As we sat in her living room, she shared about her belief in the Bible, prayer, and "channeling," by which she meant talking to ancient, dead Indians, or so she claimed. Sylvia described how she had helped many people find paths of success by connecting with these "spirits."

This intrigued me. I didn't know anything about the Bible. Nevertheless, I could sense something powerful working in her life. I wondered if she would be able to help me find answers to my questions, so I scheduled an appointment to come back for a personal consultation.

Just a few weeks after our initial meeting I stood alone on the doorstep of Sylvia's house. As I knocked on the door, I felt a bit nervous, not knowing what to expect. In fact, as I glanced around, I remember how the whole scene seemed a little creepy. The cool air had a musky, autumn aroma. Dry, brown leaves made a rustling sound as they scurried across the lawn. The sun hung low in the sky, making long, dark shadows that danced on the ground as the wind swept through the trees.

When Sylvia opened the door, she greeted me in a professional manner. We walked into a bedroom that she kept prepared as her office. She lit some candles on what looked like a little altar, then she sat down and explained the process.

"I'm going to contact a mighty Indian spirit who will give me insight into your life, Keith." *Hey, this will be great*, I thought, *she'll give me the inside scoop—some real help*. With a serious look on her face she next gave me a warning, "Now, don't be surprised at what might happen." She explained how, once—as a friend of hers had done the same thing for a client—spirits materialized in the form of little ranting demons. Her friend and the client chased the little demons all around the house until finally cornering them in the bathroom. Then Sylvia finished the story by telling me that the demons had escaped by going down the toilet.

I really didn't know what to think about that—demons down the toilet? What was I getting myself into here? Now I really felt curious and somewhat anxious about what would happen next.

As she began to contact what she said was an ancient dead Indian, she took a deep breath and shut her eyes. Her body went limp, and then it looked as if someone touched her with a live electrical wire, as a series of shock waves raced through her body.

Then, as she sat motionless in her chair, suddenly, her eyes popped open and she looked straight at me. At a steady pace and in a concerned, even tone, she explained, "You have a problem. You are possessed by two disincarnates." (She believed "disincarnates" were spirits waiting around for reincarnation.) To this she added, "And they're female." Stunned, I sat back and thought, *So, you're telling me that I have two women who can't get along living inside of me?*

All this became too much for me—chasing demons down the toilet and being possessed by two female spirits. When our session finished, I politely thanked her. However, having gotten no real answers, I never went back.

I continued to search for answers as to why things weren't working out the way I planned. I kept thinking, *There must be a better way to live.* Because the channeler had prayed to Jesus and read the Bible, I started thinking more about God, but that just raised more questions: Did God have a plan for my life? Would He help me pay my rent, find a better job, or meet the right woman to marry? If I followed Jesus, would I become wealthy and stay healthy, never suffer financially or be diagnosed with cancer? What kind of person might I become if I followed Jesus? What would He expect from me?

I can remember, as a child, reciting a simple prayer before the family meal; "Thank You for our milk and bread, and people who are kind and good. Amen." Nevertheless, as I grew into my teen years, our family phased out offering words of thanks before our meals. It just made sense to us at that time. Our sporadic church attendance also had come to an end. So, like many other American youth, religion would not hinder my choices to become all that I wanted to be.

I can recall two experiences that reveal a drastic change that occurred in my teen years. The first experience happened when I was just ten years old during a family vacation to the Rocky Mountains. We stayed in one of a group of about a dozen rustic duplex cabins nestled among the towering, majestic peaks. I can still remember the constant roar of the boulder-strewn, cold and frothing white water of the river in the valley.

Among the other families vacationing at the cabins, there happened to be a boy about my age, and he had brought his wrist-rocket slingshot. He hiked around the cabins practicing on birds with deadly accuracy.

Walking around the camp I found delicately feathered creatures with stones embedded in them. Seeing the dead birds made my heart sink. The needless loss of life moved my young heart to have funerals for the lifeless, limp little birds. At this tender age, I responded with love and compassion to the senseless killing of these little creatures. In time, however, my heart would change.

Some eight years later, I remember an incident that happened while out hunting in the Iowa countryside with my buddies. My friends carried shotguns, and I had a .22-caliber rifle. As we walked through some dry grass on the edge of a wooded area, I spotted a sparrow in a small tree about twenty feet away. Staring down the sights of the rifle, I carefully lined up the little creature in the sights and slowly pulled the trigger. The bullet flew right through the target, and the sparrow fell to the ground in a lifeless tumble. We walked over to inspect the kill. "That bird didn't even know what hit it," a friend said, and we all laughed. My earlier love for living things had become paralyzed.

My condition had even become obvious to those around me. I can remember how even the thought of saying, "I love you," made me feel far too vulnerable. In fact, I held back those words from my parents at the end of phone conversations and even when we gathered for the holidays.

Of course, my experience is not unique. Paralyzed love has become an epidemic in our society. When you visit a favorite news website, how many stories reveal incidents brought on by paralyzed love?

How else, for example, could we explain the story of seventeen-year-old, straight-A student Lesha Donaby? She came to visit her cousin in a mid-sized, midwestern town that was not known for violence, and she left in a coffin.

Lesha and a friend were passengers in the car her cousin was driving. A car in front of them stopped as they turned a corner near her cousin's house. Her cousin waited a bit, honked the horn, and then drove around the stopped car, continuing on down the street to her house, where she parked and the girls got out.

The car that her cousin had honked at had followed them. After an exchange of words, a man got out of the car and started shooting. Lesha was shot several times. She stumbled into her cousin's house and said, "I'm hit, I'm hit, I'm dying." A short time later, she died at a local hospital. The man's mentality said, "If you honk, you deserve to die," which reveals a paralyzed love (*Wichita Eagle*, July 2–7, 2008).

The results of paralyzed love surround us; murders, rapes, burglaries, drug addiction, extortion, and domestic abuse, not to mention the lies, affairs, abusive bosses, quarrels, and family feuds that never make the news. I lived with a paralyzed love and did not understand or acknowledge my hard heart.

In Chapter Two, I will begin to explain how discovering the power of goodness led me to find the answers to my deepest questions. The answers I received helped my love to become functional and healthy.

Chapter Two

A New Beginning

Until I reached twenty-seven years of age, my life was all about playing the guitar. Some of the beautiful guitars in my collection included Ramirez and Mattingly classical guitars, a Silver Anniversary Fender Stratocaster, a blond Gibson 335, and a synthesizer guitar with a Kawai sound module. I also owned a PA system with JBL speakers, a Fender Twin guitar amplifier, a Rockman headphone guitar amplifier, and a Roland JC-55 guitar amplifier with many, many sound effects.

I started playing the classical guitar when I was twelve. By the age of seventeen, I was accepted to play in master classes with well-known classical guitarists like Christopher Parkening and Pepe Romero. By the age of eighteen, I was practicing four to six hours a day. I studied the classical guitar at the University of Missouri-Kansas (UMKC) Conservatory of Music in Kansas City, Missouri, and then transferred to the University of Georgia.

My life embraced music. I had no time for religion—even when my health was threatened. While studying at the University of Georgia, a dermatologist discovered that I had an odd-looking mole. After the biopsy report came back, my physician informed me that I could have malignant melanoma, a dangerous type of skin cancer. He recommended removing more of the tissue surrounding the suspicious mole.

I soon found myself lying on a hard and cold examination table, receiving multiple injections of an anesthetic. My right side just above the hip bone became numb. I felt only a slight pressure as the scalpel cut through my skin. The surgeon compassionately inquired, "How are you doing?"

> *I had no urge to seek my Creator in prayer. It simply never occurred to me that I should, or even could, pray.*

With my eyes tightly shut, I muttered, "I'm okay. I'm counting to pass the time." In the lonely darkness of my mind, as the surgeon sliced through my flesh, removing a possible cancer, I focused my thoughts on numbers. I had no urge to seek my Creator in prayer. It simply never occurred to me that I should, or even could, pray. When I received the final report from the biopsy and it showed no other sign of cancer, I offered no prayer of thanksgiving to God.

Not until five years after my scare with cancer did I begin to think more seriously about my life. I had become frustrated with the journey down the road of life and began asking questions, such as, *Why don't things ever work out for me? I'm a good person. Why does life have to be so hard?* Repeatedly I thought, *There must be a better way to live.* Just a few months after my experience with the "Christian channeler," I met a man named Maurice who would help me find answers to questions I did not even know I needed to ask.

At that time, I needed to make some extra money, so I rented a booth at a flea market on the weekends. As a professional musician, I owned a lot of equipment, some which I sold. I also traveled around to pawnshops, looking to buy musical equipment for re-sale.

On Sunday mornings—even on cold days or when he had a busy schedule—Maurice would stop by to visit. He was closer to my dad's age than to mine, but the difference in age didn't matter. We became friends. Maurice didn't try to correct me as I opened up and shared my challenges with him. Rather, he sympathized, telling me about some of his own mistakes and about challenges in his own life.

Above all, I noticed that Maurice seemed satisfied and content. He didn't project an obsession with personal accomplishments or material possessions. We would sit on the tailgate of my pickup truck at the flea market and talk for hours.

After about eight weeks of visiting on Sundays, he invited me to his home for dinner and a Bible study. A good home-cooked meal always piques the interest of a bachelor, but I did feel a little hesitant about going to a Bible study. Nevertheless, something deep inside compelled me to accept his invitation.

I'll never forget my first evening visiting with Maurice and his family in their home. I would describe the experience as being completely the opposite of what I'd experienced at the channeler's home. It did not feel creepy at all. For the first time, I experienced a Christian home in action. They actually used the Bible like a reference book to get answers to their questions in life. Maurice's wife, Nancy, had a joyous perspective on life that could not be shaken. Their three children even looked forward to the Bible study.

I had never heard anyone pray the way this family did. They opened their hearts to God, prayed for me, prayed for each other, asking for forgiveness for their mistakes and for His strength to live each day. Never before had I encountered a family with such humility and openness.

As they admitted their mistakes and challenges, it made a powerful impression upon my mind. They did not consider themselves victims but tried to learn and grow from life's challenges. Before I met Maurice's family, I'd thought of Christians as hypocrites. However, to my surprise, I could not detect any kind of a pretentious spirit in Maurice's family.

They were not ruled by a list of "do's and don'ts." They simply tried to embrace the teachings of Jesus as their model. Their relationship with God appealed to me, so I kept coming back week after week for dinner and a Bible study.

For the first time in my life, I began to pray and read the Bible and, to my surprise, started getting answers to my questions. Slowly, I began to realize how often selfishness had motivated my choices. I realized how I had dealt with people in a rude and sometimes abrasive manner.

For the first time, I viewed my stubbornness as a liability instead of an asset, and I saw my compulsion to spend a night partying as a selfish desire that was making a fool of me. I acknowledged my true motives in the light of God's goodness and asked Him to show me more. For the first time in my life, I realized that I needed help.

So how did I receive healing for my "live my life my way" paralyzed love? The same way that a paralyzed man received healing from Jesus. On one occasion, Jesus taught in a house more crowded than a Wal-Mart giving away free televisions the day after Thanksgiving. Then four men arrived at the house carrying their paralyzed friend on a mat and found such a great crowd they could not get him inside. So, his friends took him up on the roof, tore a hole in the roof and lowered their companion into Jesus' presence. As the dust settled, everyone in the house paused, waiting for Jesus' response to this brazen intrusion. With a look that revealed He knew the man's heart, Jesus—the Son of God and Creator of this world—exclaimed, "Son, your sins are forgiven!"

I can imagine a peaceful glow spreading across the man's face as he lay motionless before Jesus. He received at that moment what I had been missing and yet longed for during my teenage years—hearing my Creator proclaim to me, "Son, your sins are forgiven."

The goodness of Jesus' forgiveness empowered the process of healing my paralyzed love. His goodness brought forgiveness that produced freedom—freedom to live out the life He dreamed for me. I discovered that Jesus lived, died, and now lives to forgive me, and give me freedom. Hebrews 7:25 says, "Therefore he is able to save completely those who come to God through him, because he always lives to intercede for them."

As Jesus answered my questions, I understood that driving down the road of life with the accelerator to the floor created problems and made me vulnerable—vulnerable to misunderstanding God and my own desires and vulnerable to hurting myself and others. The Bible helped me realize that, if I had lived in the time of Christ, I could have been one of the people who mocked Jesus, pulled out His beard and spat on Him. If I had been in the crowd at Jesus' trial, I could have joined them in yelling, "Crucify Him!" (Mark 15:13–14).

I longed for God's promises to become real in my life as they had been in Maurice's life. Often I read the promise in Philippians 2:13, "For it is God who works in you to will and to act in order to fulfill His good purpose." As this promise became a reality, Jesus planted a new way of thinking deep in my soul. The Bible refers to this infusion of new thoughts as the *new heart*. "I will give you a new heart and put a new spirit in you; I will remove from you your heart of stone and give you a heart of flesh." (Ezek. 36:26) Kind words instead of cuss words came out of my mouth to a slow cashier and to a troubled co-worker. Life became a journey instead of a race to win. Jesus had answered my questions, *Why don't things work out for me?* and *Why does life have to be so hard?* He answered my questions by helping me to embrace His goodness.

Saying "yes" to His goodness became my commitment and challenge. My question, *Why don't things ever work out for me?* turned into the prayer request, *Please, Lord, help me by Your wisdom, guidance, strength and courage.*

Today, I praise God that I didn't continue down the back alley of spiritualism with Sylvia, the channeler. The Bible maps out a relationship with God—not with ancient dead Indians. In fact, after studying the Bible, I discovered that spiritualism (which involves talking to the dead) is not healthy (Deut. 18:10–12). The Lord says He detests this because we are actually talking to demons.

I still enjoy playing the guitar to this day, but for a better reason: to glorify God instead of myself. It feels great to put all those years of training and practice to good use. Jesus opened the door for me to receive a bachelor's degree in theology with a minor in biblical languages and a master's degree in pastoral ministry. I love living the life He specifically designed for me.

I can tell you this: Jesus has an awesome plan for your life. He is *for* you, not *against* you; He loves you and will not abandon you. His strength can make up for your weakness. His peace can settle your unrest. He wants you on His team. He accepts you today and wants to walk with you through life. He will answer the deepest questions you have in your soul.

You have done nothing in the past that He does not know about or understand. Your life is an open book to Him—your mistakes, your failures, your accomplishments, and your victories. He knows it all. He seeks to help you understand more about His way of thinking, and to embrace His joy, fun and peace each day of your life.

He desires to give you hope when you are frustrated or discouraged and to provide the healing of forgiveness that will sooth your soul.

What made the difference for me? What changed my life? Getting answers to the deepest questions in my heart, and—without Jesus' help—I would not have even known what questions I needed to ask. Do you have a desire to discover the deepest questions in your heart that demand an answer?

Chapter Three

Seeking Goodness

Jesus can answer the deepest questions in our hearts that must be answered, and yet we all face a big challenge—how to get the answers. To get them requires that we accept Jesus as the authority in our lives. Yet most people struggle to welcome Him as the One with authority. Some people simply reject His existence; others reject Him because they think that accepting Jesus as an authority means accepting Him as the dictator of their lives. If this was true, then we would be forced to endure a rigid, restrictive, never-have-any-fun life as we waited for heaven. However, neither of these perspectives has the right view of the character of Jesus. To reveal what it means to accept Jesus as the authority in our lives, I would like to share a story that happened to me in one of the first churches in which I served as a pastor.

The story began when my wife, Ann, started to study the Bible with a woman I'll call Samantha. Samantha's heart burned with a desire to know more about Jesus. As she discovered more, His love became embedded deep in her soul, and, as a result she decided to be baptized.

Her husband, whom we'll call Nick, also possessed a deep interest in spirituality. However, his passion took a different direction. He preferred to be involved with a New Age organization that practiced transcendental meditation.

When Nick learned about Samantha's upcoming baptism, he supported her desire to be baptized and requested to be baptized himself. As we talked about his baptism, I explained that it would be best if he waited until he believed some of the teachings of the Bible, such as the teaching that Jesus died to be our Savior.

On the day of Samantha's baptism, a dozen roses filled a vase in the sanctuary. The aroma of food for the fellowship meal wafted through the air. The congregation sang hymns, as I stepped down into the baptistery. Helping Samantha into the water, I noticed that Nick stood up and walked toward the front of the sanctuary.

I shared with the congregation a few words about Samantha's experience with Jesus. As I turned to get a better position for the baptism, it startled me to see Nick, standing near the edge of the baptistery behind a wall so that the congregation could not see him. I thought, *Hey, this is great; he wants to get a closer look.*

I got to say those wonderful words, "I baptize you in the name of the Father, the Son, and the Holy Spirit." Then I helped Samantha lean back as she disappeared under the water and surfaced with a big smile. When she stepped out of the baptistery, Nick popped out from behind the wall into full view of the congregation. He stood before everyone, perched on the ledge of the baptistery and, in a loud voice proclaimed, "I so much appreciate Keith and Ann's ministry to my wife and me, but I do not accept any human authority, so I baptize myself." Then he knelt down, white linen suit and all, rolled over onto his back and plunged into the baptistery with a big splash. He sank to the bottom of the water, where he remained for what seemed like minutes. When he finally surfaced and stepped out of the water, I beheld a sight I had never seen before: a man who just baptized himself, now wearing a soaking wet suit and tie.

What odd thing happened here? Well, it's like this. Without accepting Jesus as our authority, we won't embrace His goodness that empowers us to accept a relationship with Him; instead, we will find a way to define our own relationship with Jesus. But before we can begin to understand God's answers, we need to accept Him as our authority. When Nick stated that he did not accept any human authority, he did not realize that the real issue he faced was if He would accept God as his authority.

To explain from the Bible what it means to accept Jesus as the authority for our lives, I would like to start with the best-known, most famous verse in the Bible, John 3:16. This verse comes in the middle of a conversation that Jesus had with Nicodemus, a Pharisee and religious leader among the Jews. I believe Nicodemus recognized Jesus' words as important when he heard them, although he probably never imagined that they would often become the first words of Jesus that a child would memorize or that they would be referenced with a big "JOHN 3:16" sign at football games.

Jesus wanted Nicodemus to know more about His goodness when He said, "For God so loved the world that he gave his one and only Son, that whoever believes in him shall not perish but have eternal life" (John 3:16). When you read this passage in the Bible (which I did not do until I was twenty-seven years of age), you will notice that this verse 16 repeats the words of John 3:15. Verse 15 says, "… that everyone who believes may have eternal life in him." Yet, verse 15 is the last half of the sentence. The first half of the sentence (John 3:14) says, "Just as Moses lifted up the snake in the wilderness, so the Son of Man must be lifted up." This means the foundation for the most famous verse in the Bible comes from a snake story found in the Old Testament!

In Numbers 21:4–9, we find this biblical story of the Israelites leaving Egypt and blaming God and Moses for all their troubles. The Lord told Moses to make a snake and put it on a pole so that those who were bitten could look at the snake and live. As a religious leader in Jesus' day, Nicodemus would have known all about the "snake being lifted up" in the wilderness. Now Jesus was going to use this to teach Nicodemus a new truth about His purpose for Nicodemus' life.

In the biblical story, the people of Israel had become impatient. Fatigue had set in after they had been set free from slavery in Egypt. They started to complain about everything. Their expectations had not been met. Nothing seemed to be going as they planned. Have you ever been there—with everything being bad and nothing going right?

God then responded to their complaints and things got even worse! How about that? Have you ever felt as if your prayers bounced off the ceiling and, just when you thought things could not get any worse, they did? When, in their disappointment, the people of Israel sought sympathy and compassion for their difficulties, God made things worse. We have to ask, "Why would God do that?"

Numbers 21:5, 6 describes what happened: "…they spoke against God and against Moses, and said, 'Why have you brought us up out of Egypt to die in the wilderness? There is no bread! There is no water! And we detest this miserable food!' Then the LORD sent venomous snakes among them; they bit the people and many Israelites died."

How could God, who healed the lepers and made the blind to see and the deaf to hear respond in such a way to His people? To understand the answer to this dilemma means that we grasp what Jesus tried to teach Nicodemus about His role in Nicodemus' life.

Returning to the Old Testament account, it says: "The LORD said to Moses, 'Make a snake and put it up on a pole; anyone who is bitten can look at it and live'" (Num. 21:8). God simply said to the Israelites, "Look and live."

In the midst of their complaining, the people of Israel had forgotten God. They believed the snakes represented an unsolvable problem. God gave them a solution that meant they would need to yield to God by looking at the snake on a pole. Jesus wanted Nicodemus to understand that he had the same problem as the Israelites, in that he would not "look and live." Deep in his heart, he had a problem with yielding to God as the authority.

Jesus wanted Nicodemus to embrace the same "look and live" solution. What did God require for healing in the Israelite camp? Simply to look—to look at a bronze snake on a pole. Can you imagine being in the Israelite camp, being bitten by a snake—a bite which would bring certain death—and not looking? It is hard to imagine, but it happened.

What kind of a "look" did it take for a cure? Certainly more than a casual look. Not like the looking you do when visiting a zoo or a botanical garden on a Sunday afternoon, but more like the way you would look on the Internet for information after your two-year-old has accidentally eaten twelve aspirin tablets. You would look at those instructions with your full attention. A life depends upon the looking!

Before we can look with this kind of intentionality, we must yield to the one giving the instructions as being the authority. Could you imagine calling a local tire center to ask what to do if your child swallowed several handfuls of aspirin tablets? On the other hand, would you argue with the instructions given to you by Poison Control as you looked at your two-year-old child unconscious on the floor? Not if you accepted Poison Control as an authority.

In the episode with the snakes, God desired to show the Israelites that He had authority and could provide real help, if they would do their part by looking to Him. To receive healing, all they had to do was look. To look meant they realized their need of what only He could give. To look meant accepting God as the authority. Jesus wanted Nicodemus to know that to accept Him as the authority meant that He would be his provider. The Israelites complained and things got worse. Then God sent a solution that revealed He had authority over snakes and would provide real help.

I have observed that, through determination and will power, people can live what most would call a good life, a life they enjoy. However, a strong, determined self-will does not lead people to accept Jesus as the ultimate authority in their lives and look to Him for help.

The Bible presents a radical plan for our lives. It challenges us to accept Him as the authority, which means we must live each day by asking for His help. For example, we need to ask for His help to treat others the way we would like to be treated, to even love our enemies. In Matthew 5:44–46, Jesus said, "But I tell you, love your enemies and pray for those who persecute you, that you may be children of your Father in heaven. He causes his sun to rise on the evil and the good, and sends rain on the righteous and the unrighteous. If you love those who love you, what reward will you get?" To accomplish this kind of challenge, we need Jesus. This kind of radical behavior represents a miracle, not a New Year's resolution.

Jesus has a role to play in our lives that no one else can fulfill. He is the "…the author and finisher of our faith…" (Heb. 12:2, NKJV). He is the rewarder of those who seek Him, the One who can light our path, the One who works within us to will and to do for His good pleasure, the One who blots out our sins, the One who died for us that we might not perish but have eternal life. Jesus has authority yet, before He can help us, we must yield. We must look to Him to live. We can humble ourselves each day knowing that we need His help. Yet for the complaining Israelites and the proud Nicodemus that had become a problem.

Before you can look, you must yield. Before you can follow, you must accept Him as the authority. It sounds so simple. If you get bitten, just look. What do you have to lose? Why not try it?

Well, *to look* means that you yield to His authority as One who provides real help. Some people in the Israelite camp died rather than look so they could live. Can you imagine that? Yet how many people today look to Jesus for real help to live their lives? How about you? Has anything kept you from looking to Jesus as the authority so that He can provide real help that only He can give? The first basic issue in discovering the answers Jesus seeks to provide to your deepest questions is to accept Him as the authority so you will ask for His help. Then you can ask Him for help in understanding the power of His goodness.

Chapter Four

Faith

The next issue to understand about real Christianity—something that will help you get answers to your questions—is to embrace what the Bible teaches about faith. Many people today can use the word *faith* to describe having a strong will. In other words, if you just have enough faith, God will do what you want. That perspective on faith means that *you* know what you need from God, instead of realizing that *God* knows what you need. Looking at faith with this kind of *absence of doubt* perspective can make us even more demanding. That perspective means, as long as we have a strong will, not willing to doubt, then God will give us what we ask.

Sometimes people get this idea about not doubting by misapplying James 1:6–8 that says, "But when you ask, you must believe and not doubt, because the one who doubts is like a wave of the sea, blown and tossed by the wind. That person should not expect to receive anything from the Lord. Such a person is double-minded and unstable in all they do." Does this verse mean that if we doubt that Jesus will give us what we ask for, we will not receive what we ask?

Verse six starts with the words, "But when you ask…." Compare that with the preceding verse five that says, "If any of you lacks wisdom, you should ask God…" Verses 6 through 8 expand upon verse five that tells us to ask God for wisdom. These verses tell us that, when we ask for His wisdom, we should believe that He will help. So, does this Bible passage tell us that, if we ask God for something we want and do not doubt, it will then happen? No, it tells us to rely upon God's wisdom, not our own. If we believe this verse tells us that we can get what *we* want from God if we do not doubt, then that turns our not doubting into a way to manipulate God into getting what we want. This passage in James leads us to first ask God for wisdom and not doubt that He will help us by providing *His* wisdom.

Today people can have a challenge understanding what the Bible teaches about faith. Faith in Jesus means trusting in Him, and yet that does not present the complete picture. The Bible reveals an important reality we cannot afford to miss; we need Jesus' help to trust in Him. How could we self-centered humans trust in Jesus—who is totally unselfish—without His help?

I remember when I first grasped this most amazing reality. It led me to embrace the fact that I am not alone. *I* did not have to figure out every issue and problem I faced on my own. Jesus, the all-powerful Creator promised to help *me*. I quickly embraced this amazing, awesome truth after I became a Christian. It brought joy and relief to my heart as I started asking Jesus for help with everything, and, to my astonishment, He answered!

I had no idea that a life of faith meant embracing a routine of asking Him to help me trust in Him. I thought that because of all the big problems in the world, such as starving people, murders, wars, tornados, earthquakes, fires, and floods that Jesus must be way too busy to help me. And because so many things were in chaos, I thought that He did not seem to be very effective. But I discovered that my conclusions about Jesus had been wrong.

I remember an experience early in my relationship with Jesus that became a milestone for teaching me how to live with faith. It started with a loud Bang! Bang! Bang! as someone knocked on my front door. Jostled by the noise, my mind rose through layers of deep sleep. I opened one eye and saw the red glowing numbers on my clock—3:00 a.m. *Am I dreaming?* I wondered. I lay in bed for a moment; then I heard it again. Bang! Bang! Bang!

There really is someone at my door, I thought, as I tossed back the warm blankets and darted across the cold floor. Opening the door, I saw the shadowy outline of my friend Stan. Without hesitation, he burst into my apartment.

"Man, I should have listened to you. Oh, man, I should have listened to you," he moaned.

Stan, a husky fellow of about 20 years of age, lived in an adjacent apartment. Being the son of a preacher, he loved to talk about the Bible. He possessed a great sense of humor, and, if he thought you needed it, he would give you the shirt off his back.

"I shouldn't have gone to that party," he continued. "I should have listened."

"What happened?" I asked.

Stan slumped onto the couch and started to explain. "Satan got me; Satan got me bad. I got in a fight, a bad fight. Everything had been going fine. I was just downing a few beers, not bothering anyone. Then this guy came over and got in my face, looking for a fight. So I gave him one. I messed him up bad. I pounded his face in."

"Why did you do that?"

He paused, hung his head down and said in a small voice, "I don't know. I really didn't want to."

Just ten hours earlier, Stan confidently sat on the same couch and told me about how he planned to attend the party. At that time, he had a gleam in his eyes and an animated tone in his voice. He told me all about how he could handle going to this party. He had convinced himself that being surrounded by drunks would not be a problem.

I reminded Stan of a previous conversation when he had shared his conviction about leaving drugs and alcohol behind. He pushed the tension of that thought aside, got up from the couch, walked out the door, and headed for the party. I knew he would regret that decision. Unfortunately, his conviction about leaving drugs and alcohol behind usually manifested itself in the strongest way the day after spending a night taking drugs and drinking alcohol.

Not long after this experience with Stan, my boss at the company I worked for invited me to a party he hosted every year. He brewed and bottled homemade beer from a special recipe just for this annual bash.

I was twenty-eight years old and had recently become a Christian. I struggled with the decision of whether or not to go. I had been praying about it. Finally, I broke the tension by choosing to go to the party, yet not drinking any alcohol while I was there. Sounds familiar, right?

I convinced myself that it would be okay to attend the party. I thought, *I can handle it, and I need to go.* I put on my favorite sweater, brushed my hair and grabbed the keys to my truck. Then, before walking out the door, I decided to kneel down beside my bed and talk to my new friend Jesus one more time before going to the party. I asked for His help and invited Him to guide me. I rose up from prayer and decided to lie down on my bed for what I thought would be just a few minutes.

I woke up at 12:30 a.m. when the phone rang. Who might be calling at that time of night? Stan. He worked for the same company, had attended the party, and needed a ride home. By the time I arrived at my boss's house, only a few cars of lingering guests remained in the driveway. As I pulled in the driveway, Stan's dark outline approached. He clambered into the cab of my pickup truck. Instantly, the air filled with the familiar stench of beer and cigarettes.

While I chauffeured him home, the reality hit me; if I hadn't opened my heart to Jesus one more time, asking for help before going to the party, I too, could have come from the party with slurred words and a confused mind.

This experience had a huge impact on my relationship with Jesus. I realized that going to the party would have been a mistake for me. Because I stopped and asked for His help, I stayed on track with Him. I did not realize it at the time, but Jesus was teaching me how to live a life of faith.

> *Living a life of faith means living with a commitment to ask for His help. We accept His perspective on goodness as our reality.*

Just think, if Stan would have stayed in my living room and asked for Jesus' advice about his desires to attend the party, and then prayed for the Lord's help and guidance, what insight might Jesus have provided him?

I can rejoice that I had "one more prayer" before going to the party. I am so glad that Jesus gave me a special experience to understand how living a life of faith means living with a commitment to ask for His help, to ask Jesus questions. Faith means we do not live alone. We've made a commitment to accept His perspective on goodness as our reality. We can be honest, open, and vulnerable, sharing our hopes, dreams and fears with Jesus as we ask Him questions.

Jesus showed me the importance of living by faith. That became clear after I missed the party. If I would live by faith, asking for His help, He would bring the right kind of help just when I needed it the most. I also discovered that as I continued with a routine of asking for His help, my confidence in seeking Him first and following His answers grew stronger. Yet, I will never in this life graduate from needing His help.

Hebrews 11:6 provides an interesting window into how the Bible describes faith. "And without faith it is impossible to please God, because anyone who comes to him must believe that he exists and that he rewards those who earnestly seek him." This verse reveals that without faith it is impossible to relate to God. Remember, faith means we need His help to trust in Him. Therefore, we believe He exists, and we believe that He will help us as we seek Him because He has helped us to trust in Him.

One of the best passages providing a clear definition of what it means to live by faith and ask in faith does not even contain the word *faith*. "Ask and it will be given to you; seek and you will find; knock and the door will be opened to you. For everyone who asks receives; the one who seeks finds; and to the one who knocks, the door will be opened. Which of you, if your son asks for bread, will give him a stone? Or if he asks for a fish, will give him a snake? If you, then, though you are evil, know how to give good gifts to your children, how much more will your Father in heaven give good gifts to those who ask him!" (Matt. 7:7–11).

Faith means asking. Asking Him questions, asking for His help to trust in Him. It is the kind of asking that represents a regular, natural dialogue with Him throughout our day. We can talk to Him as a Friend; believe in Him as the Creator of all, and seek Him in all things. He's ready to help us with all the situations and troubles we face, in all things both big and small. Faith means we live with a commitment of asking Him for help.

If you have not understood the meaning of faith before, you can try it out for yourself, right now. You can discover the joy and freedom of living by faith—for free, at no cost to you! Just try it and see how you can get answers that empower your relationship with Jesus. Answers that make you want to keep asking for more help.

However, faith does not mean that we will always get what we want when we ask. It does not mean that, if we just do not doubt, He will give us what we want. Jesus does not seek to create in us strong, stubborn wills that are convinced we must have what we ask for and that we will receive it if we just do not doubt.

Faith means we ask for His help because we believe He knows the best thing for us. We need His help because we are born with a selfish nature, with misdirected and distorted values, hopes, and dreams. We need His input on everything. We need His wisdom, guidance, strength, and courage—all of which come to us by asking for His help to trust in Him.

Since faith means we ask for His help as a routine and awesome habit, we need to make sure that we understand how He will answer. In the next chapter, I will take a closer look at how Jesus answers as we ask Him to help us trust in Him.

CHAPTER FIVE

The Problem

Jesus delights in answering as we ask Him questions. Yet, we all face a challenge with understanding the answers He provides. It is not because He plays games with us as He answers; it is because His answers reveal His goodness, and humans can have a hard time understanding His goodness. Goodness represents His character, how He thinks and acts. If we don't understand His goodness, we can misunderstand or even ignore His answer. Then, if we don't understand His answer, we can give up on living by faith, thinking that it does not work. That represents a big problem if we want to embrace this basic element of real Christianity.

Jesus answers our request for help the only way He can—with His goodness.

The Bible reveals that faith means we trust in Jesus, yet we cannot trust in Jesus without His help. Jesus answers our request for help the only way He can—with His goodness. That means, to experience real Christianity, we not only live by asking for His help, but we also ask Him to help us understand His answers. He can help us understand His answers so then we can choose to follow (that is what it means to believe) and ask for His help to keep the commitment we made to follow His answer.

These concepts of faith (asking for help), His goodness (how He answers) and believing (choosing to follow His answer) represent basic elements that work together to form a matrix that drives a real relationship with Jesus. These three basic concepts empower Him to teach, lead, and help us to understand the plans He has for our lives. To misunderstand these elements means that we can dismiss or become confused by the answers Jesus seeks to give us, and that is a tragedy.

If you have dismissed a relationship with Jesus in the past, this is your opportunity to gain a clear understanding about how a friendship with Jesus provides real help, real answers. You can save yourself years of frustration that can come from trying to have a relationship with Jesus without understanding how faith, His goodness, and believing all work together.

If you currently have some type of a relationship with Jesus, you might have a few things to unlearn. As you unlearn the murky, commonly taught, and sometimes confusing explanations for these three concepts, you can begin to experience the freedom that comes as Jesus answers your deepest questions.

Jesus desires a relationship with us in which we ask for His help by asking questions, then let Him help us to apply His goodness to our questions so we can understand His answers, and thus choose to follow Him. A growing relationship with Jesus is a cycle of asking, applying His goodness to our question, and making a commitment to follow His answer. This matrix becomes a constant repeating cycle that allows Jesus to help us embrace the awesome plan He has for our lives.

If we do not understand His answers, how can we grow in our relationship with Him? I hope you are beginning to understand how big of an impact these basic concepts of faith, His goodness, and believing have in your relationship with Jesus.

I would like to share a story with you that helped me learn an important lesson about getting answers to our questions from Jesus. This event happened after I became a pastor, while visiting with a church member I'll call Susan.

Susan taught me an important lesson about Jesus' goodness. She had been sick with cancer for several years and had endured many difficult days in the hospital. Throughout her illness, her health always seemed to bounce back. However, one day that changed. I remember, during one of my last visits with her in the hospital, she realized the cancer might win after all. The doctors had inserted a breathing tube into her trachea because the tumor blocked her airway. As you can imagine, that made it difficult to talk. I entered her hospital room and sat down in a chair beside the bed. We started an intense conversation as she wrote on a yellow legal pad and I spoke. In big letters with quick strokes of her pen, she wrote the questions: "What did I do to deserve this?" I responded, "God isn't like that, Susan. He isn't punishing you." Then she scribbled, "The Bible says you reap what you sow." For about half an hour, our conversation continued as she poured out these painful questions from deep in her heart. I closed the visit with prayer and left feeling ineffective and heavy hearted. I yearned for Susan to understand that God would not punish her for past mistakes by giving her cancer.

Not long after the visit with the yellow legal pad, the cancer took Susan's life. Yet, before she died, I visited her several more times, and her confidence in God seemed strong. Nevertheless, the conversation with the yellow legal pad always lingered in the back of my mind.

As I prepared to conduct Susan's funeral, I thought about her life. She loved to sing hymns and could sit for hours singing while someone played the piano. After she contracted cancer, she would just sit and listen to the music, reading the lyrics. Susan made it a point to come to church with her two daughters, even though I could tell she experienced some serious pain as she sat in church.

More than 250 friends and family attended her funeral. Many people commented on Susan's faith in God. Her relationship with Jesus seemed obvious to all her friends and family, but what about that conversation with the yellow legal pad? Years later, I would come to understand how Jesus used our conversation on that day in the hospital. When I left that visit, I felt defeated, not being able to help her. Yet, I came to understand—on that day in the hospital with the yellow legal pad—that Jesus gave her just what she needed.

Susan needed someone to listen, not tell her what to think. She needed to get those painful questions out in the open, which she did as we talked. As she got her questions out in the open, over time, it provided an opportunity for Jesus to give her the answers she needed. While I did not have the words to answer her questions, eventually Jesus did.

Susan had been honest with God. She had faith. She didn't have time for a sugar-coated relationship with Jesus. She allowed me to witness her vulnerability with God. I did not understand at that time that Jesus wanted her to get her painful questions out in the open so He could answer those questions from deep in her heart before she died. My role in the visit did not include answering her questions. Jesus just wanted me to help her get those deep questions that had been blistering her soul out in the open, so He could then work to provide her the answers.

The path to understanding the depth of Jesus' goodness for us starts by being vulnerable, being honest with Jesus, and getting the deepest questions in our souls out of our hearts and into the hands of Jesus. He wants to meet us where we live—in the real world of frustration, disappointment, and anger that can result from overdue bills, bypassed promotions, failed marriages, rude bosses, expensive auto repairs, and unemployment. When we are willing to be honest with God and ask Jesus the real questions in the depth of our souls—as Susan did on that day we visited in the hospital—then Jesus can help us accept His answers, answers that reflect His goodness.

I hope by now you are beginning to understand that what you do *not* know can help you if you are willing to learn. You can experience getting real answers to your deepest questions and experience real Christianity. The next chapter begins to show you how the process of getting answers to your questions can work in your life.

Chapter Six

An Example

Jesus' encounter with a man who has become known as "the rich young ruler" reveals that, in addition to our honesty challenge with Jesus, we can encounter another problem when seeking to understand Jesus' answers to our questions. The story begins in Mark 10:17 when a man interrupts Jesus. "As Jesus started on his way, a man ran up to him and fell on his knees before him. 'Good teacher,' he asked, 'what must I do to inherit eternal life?'"

The man asked an important question, "What must I do to inherit eternal life?" We should all ask Jesus that question. As He often did, Jesus answered his question with another question. "Why do you call me good?" Then He expanded upon His answer, saying, "No one is good—except God alone. You know the commandments: 'You shall not murder, you shall not commit adultery, you shall not steal, you shall not give false testimony, you shall not defraud, honor your father and mother" (Mark 10:18–19).

Jesus quoted some of the Ten Commandments in His answer to the man. Yet, He first asked, "Why do you call me good?" Why did Jesus first focus on that part of what the man said? Did Jesus ignore His bombshell of a question about what he must do to inherit eternal life? I believe Jesus sought to direct the man's attention toward an understanding of His goodness.

The Bible tells us that Jesus has a love- or goodness-based perspective as He interacts with us. In fact, we can describe His character or way of thinking as always good. Consider one of many verses that describes Jesus as love: "Whoever does not love does not know God, because God is love" (1John 4:8). This verse lets us know that if we do not know Jesus' goodness, we do not know Him. That's why Jesus asked the man, "Why do you call me good," after he had asked Jesus, "Good teacher, what must I do to inherit eternal life?"

Since Jesus' love defines what is good, accepting His goodness forms a vital part of the foundation for our relationship with Him. What Jesus told the man next makes perfect sense. Jesus quoted some of the Ten Commandments because the Ten Commandments help us understand His goodness.

In Romans 3:20, the Bible tells us, "Therefore no one will be declared righteous [good] in God's sight by the works of the law; rather, through the law we become conscious of our sin." The book of Romans informs us that the Ten Commandments cannot be used as a means of salvation. This means the Ten Commandments do not represent a daily to-do list to qualify for heaven. The Ten Commandments make us conscious of our mistakes as we become aware of Jesus' perspective on goodness.

The Commandments help us to realize how the Holy Spirit will be working in our hearts to create goodness and help us to choose His goodness. The Ten Commandments help us to become aware of what's good so that we want to know more. In that way, we come to understand how much we need Jesus. Jesus said, "Nevertheless I tell you the truth. It is to your advantage that I go away; for if I do not go away, the Helper will not come to you; but if I depart, I will send Him to you. And when He has come, He will convict the world of sin, and of righteousness, and of judgment" (John 16:7–8, NKJV). By combining Romans 3:20 and John 16:7–8, we can understand that the Advocate, the Holy Spirit, also called *the Comforter*, will help us become aware of our sin through the Ten Commandments.

In answering the man's question with the Ten Commandments, Jesus wanted to know if he understood the role of the Ten Commandments in his life. The man next told Jesus something revealing, "...All these I have kept since I was a boy" (Mark 10:20). What a statement! The man thought of Jesus' goodness as a list of things to do, and that's a problem. He did not understand Jesus' answer to his first question because he had not embraced what God wanted to teach him about His goodness. He looked at a relationship with God as a list of things to do, instead of a journey in which we learn more about Jesus' way of thinking. Jesus did not just want to give him a list of the right things to do. Jesus wanted to help him understand why His unselfish way of thinking always represented the best option.

> *By offering him treasure in heaven in exchange for treasure on earth, Jesus addressed the rich young ruler's real problem.*

So, with the man's "to-do list" response in mind, Jesus gave him something outrageous to do. I believe Jesus did this with the intention of providing him with an opportunity to learn more about His goodness. "Jesus looked at him and loved him. 'One thing you lack,' he said. 'Go, sell everything you have and give to the poor, and you will have treasure in heaven. Then come, follow me'" (Mark 10:21).

Jesus looked at him, loved him, and gave the man something "over the top" to do. Jesus created a dilemma for the man by telling him to sell all and follow Him or keep his stuff and stay home. Jesus challenged his perspective on a relationship with God. The man looked at a relationship with God from a "just do the right thing" perspective. So, Jesus presented him with the opportunity of selling all his things as the "right thing" to do. Jesus' answer created a problem for the man.

The problem was that this man, who had great wealth and became known as the "rich young ruler," did not understand Jesus' goodness. So, he did not understand Jesus' answer to his question and did not know how to respond to His request to go and sell all His belongings. When Jesus highlighted the Ten Commandments, that should have given him a clue to an important reality—that the Ten Commandments reveal God's goodness and are not a way to qualify for heaven. Yet, the rich young ruler did not understand this reality.

If the rich young ruler had known about Jesus' goodness, his response to Jesus would not have been, "Teacher, all these things I have kept since I was a boy" (Mark 10:20). Instead, He could have said something like, "Only God is good and only God can empower those who do good." In saying this, he would have acknowledged that he understood and had experienced the power of Jesus' love.

It's interesting that the rich young ruler focused on only half of what Jesus told him. He focused on the *what to do* part. Jesus told him, "…Go, sell everything you have and give to the poor, and you will have treasure in heaven" (Mark 10:21). Because the rich young ruler believed that wealth represents evidence of a correct relationship with God and that you get to heaven by doing the right thing, he did not understand Jesus' answer. By offering him treasure in heaven in exchange for treasure on earth, Jesus addressed the rich young ruler's real problem.

What did the rich young ruler do? "At this the man's face fell. He went away sad, because he had great wealth" (Mark 10:22). What a missed opportunity! If the rich young ruler had embraced Jesus' goodness—even a little—he could have asked Jesus another question, such as, "Why would you tell me to go and sell all my things?" Then he would have gotten another answer, one based on Jesus' goodness. As he asked more questions and received more answers, he would have received more reasons to trust in, to believe in, and to choose to make a commitment to follow Jesus.

This simple truth becomes evident in this story. We can't make a commitment to trust in Jesus without answers to our questions. We need to ask questions, then understand how Jesus answers our questions based on His goodness. We can then make a commitment to follow His way of thinking, which means we believe the answer He provided. Next, we need to ask for His help to follow through on our commitment. If the rich young ruler had chosen to agree with Jesus' request to sell all his belongings, he could have received strength from God to follow through on selling everything. Please remember, we all have issues, yet we do not all have the same challenge as the rich young ruler. So that means this encounter does not represent a "one-size-fits-all" instruction for everyone to sell all they have before they can follow Jesus. When we put the issues we face into questions, asking Jesus, "Please help me to understand your answer," it opens up an opportunity for Him to help us embrace His love, His goodness, and His way of thinking.

In the passage after the encounter with the rich young ruler, Jesus had an interesting exchange with His disciples. In Mark 10:24–26, it says, "The disciples were amazed at his words. But Jesus said again, 'Children, how hard it is to enter the kingdom of God! It is easier for a camel to go through the eye of a needle than for someone who is rich to enter the kingdom of God.' The disciples were even more amazed, and said to each other, 'Who then can be saved?'" This question is similar to the rich young ruler's original question of "What must I do to inherit eternal life?" Jesus provided an answer based on His goodness, "...With man this is impossible, but not with God; all things are possible with God" (Mark 10:27).

> *Jesus delights in teaching us more about how His goodness applies to our lives.*

Jesus revealed that, with His help, we can learn to understand and embrace His goodness. Jesus can help us understand why His way is the best alternative, and He can give us the strength to follow the answers He provides. He delights in teaching us more about how His goodness applies to our lives.

At this time, the disciples believed that wealthy people enjoyed blessings from God and poor people were rejected. Jesus let them know that we cannot use wealth to gauge our relationship with Him. In fact, wealth can be a stumbling block for some, like the rich young ruler. However, Jesus' point was not that all wealthy people need to sell all their belongings to have a relationship with Him. His point was that, just as a large animal, like a camel, cannot fit through the eye of a needle, so someone who does not trust in Jesus' goodness cannot fit into the unselfish atmosphere of heaven.

The rich young ruler had not taken the time to learn about God's goodness. That meant he did not understand the answer Jesus gave to his question, "...What must I do to inherit eternal life?" (Mark 10:17) as an invitation to follow Him. And so, instead of telling Jesus, "...All these I have kept since I was a boy" (Mark 10:20), he should have asked Jesus, "Please help me understand your goodness."

In the next chapter, you will learn more about how to embrace Jesus' answers to your questions and how we can understand and choose the answers He gives to our deepest questions in life.

Chapter Seven

Goodness

We can understand Jesus' answers to our questions as He helps us understand and experience His goodness. With that in mind, it would seem that asking for help from our Creator to experience the power of His goodness would be every follower's delight. Yet I have found that many hesitate to ask Him for this kind of help. Why would this be the case?

To gain insights into this dilemma, let's start with a story in John, chapter 6, called "the feeding of the five thousand." Jesus fed what could have been a crowd of ten to fifteen thousand people, and He did it using only five small barley loaves and two fish. The number five thousand represents the number of men present; certainly there could have been another five to ten thousand people fed if women and children had been included in the count.

The story continues as Jesus encounters a group of people who had been present when He fed all those people, yet they had been separated after the meal. When they found Jesus, they asked Him, "'…Rabbi, when did you get here?' Jesus answered, 'Very truly I tell you, you are looking for me, not because you saw the signs I performed but because you ate the loaves and had your fill'" (John 6:25,26). These people searched for Jesus because they wondered if every seminar came with a free lunch.

Knowing their motive, Jesus told them, "Do not work for food that spoils, but for food that endures to eternal life, which the Son of Man will give you. For on him God the Father has placed his seal of approval" (John 6:27). Jesus corrected them for missing the message that leads to eternal life and for just seeking for food that perishes.

They then asked Jesus, "What must we do to do the works God requires?" (John 6:28). Notice that they had more interest in doing the right thing than understanding His message. The rich young ruler had the same problem. Jesus then said, "The work of God is this: to believe in the one he has sent" (John 6:29).

Jesus wanted them to believe His message, to take Him up on His offer of a relationship, to accept His help, to understand His goodness—instead of just seeking Him as a source for free lunches and to provide a list of the right things to do. They used the "do-the-right-thing" approach as a way to brush off the need to understand His goodness.

Next, they asked Jesus, "What sign then will you give that we may see it and believe you? What will you do?" (John 6:30). Basically, they asked Him, "Okay, you want us to believe, to make a commitment to what you teach, but how can we do that without a sign?" Can you hear the tension building in this conversation? Jesus told them they needed to accept His message that leads to eternal life, and they told Him they needed a sign before they would consider what He had to say.

Then they said, "Our ancestors ate the manna in the wilderness; as it is written: 'He gave them bread from heaven to eat'" (John 6:31). That referred to a biblical story in which God performed a miracle by providing Israel with food (manna) in the wilderness after their exodus from Egypt. Jesus next drew their attention to the message in the story. He stated, "Very truly I tell you, it is not Moses who has given you the bread from heaven, but it is my Father who gives you the true bread from heaven" (John 6:32).

Jesus connected the story about the manna in the wilderness with the miracle of feeding the people with five barley loaves and two fish. Yet, the people who asked for a sign did not understand the message in the miracle of the manna story and what it revealed about God. In the same way, they did not understand the message Jesus gave or the miracle He performed with the loaves and two fish.

Jesus then had an exchange of words with them in which He tried to teach them how they could understand His message. He said, "For the bread of God is the bread that comes down from heaven and gives life to the world. 'Sir,' they said, 'always give us this bread.' Then Jesus declared, 'I am the bread of life. Whoever comes to me will never go hungry, and whoever believes in me will never be thirsty. But as I told you, you have seen me and still you do not believe'" (John 6:33–36). Jesus summarized how they could understand His message when He said, "I am the bread of life" (John 3:35).

In what way does accepting Jesus as the bread of life reveal how He can help us understand His goodness and thus understand His message? Consider this, when we eat bread it sustains us, giving us health and life. Without food we will become weak and sick, and then die. As the bread of life, Jesus sustains our spiritual life. Just as we need to eat food each day to be healthy, we need the enrichment that comes from eating the bread of life each day to be complete and healthy spiritually. The bread of life represents Jesus' words, and His Word gives us life. That sounds simple. So why is it a challenge for people to live with Jesus as their bread of life?

The bread of life represents Jesus' words, the Bible. Yet, living with Jesus as our bread of life is not just about reading the Bible every day. It *is possible* to read the Bible every day and yet not learn about His goodness. Remember, the message and the miracle go together. Jesus fed all those people with five loaves and two fish to help them understand His message. In the same way, we need the miracle that Jesus offers us as we read His Word if we want to understand His message.

Jesus performs a miracle in our hearts each day when we ask for His help to trust in Him. He provides the gifts we need to understand His goodness. Then, as we read His Word, He can deepen our understanding of the gifts He provides. The Word of God is the bread of life that can be compared to the manna in the wilderness in the Old Testament and to the loaves and fish in the of the feeding of the five thousand in the New Testament. Just as Jesus created food in these two stories, as we take in the Word of God (the bread of life) He can create and empower His goodness in our hearts.

> *To understand His goodness we must do more than read about it in the Bible; we must do more than understand His Word as a mental exercise. We must experience His goodness in our hearts.*

He promises to create the goodness He describes in His Word within our hearts—the miracle and the message go together. As He creates His goodness in our hearts, we can understand His message. If we do not receive the miracle of having Him create His gifts in our hearts, we will not understand His message. His message will not be real to us. We need to experience the power of His goodness in our hearts to understand His goodness.

To help us understand and experience His goodness, Jesus provides the gifts of love, joy, peace, patience, kindness, goodness, gentleness, hope, compassion, courage, wisdom and self-control in our hearts. As our all-powerful Creator, Jesus can create peace in our hearts just as He created the sun, moon, stars, the trees, plants, animals and us. So, to understand His goodness we must do more than read about it in the Bible; we must do more than understand His Word as a mental exercise. We must experience the power of His goodness in our hearts as we read. That is what it means to accept Jesus as the bread of life.

Living with Jesus as our bread of life means we invite Him to create His goodness in our hearts and thus we become able to understand His message. Just as with the people that saw the miracle of the feeding of the five thousand and failed to understand, so we can fail to understand the message unless we experience the gifts He seeks to give us. To understand His answers, He must create His goodness in our hearts.

So here is the dilemma: unless we read the Word with a prayerful, open, seeking heart, asking for His help and accepting His gifts, we can miss the miracle that leads to the meaning of the message—just as the "ancestors who ate the manna in the wilderness" (John 6:49) missed the miracle and did not understand Moses' message. The people who followed Jesus and asked for a sign after Jesus fed all the people with five loaves and two fish missed the miracle that illustrated how He could be our provider of a new life.

Why do some people miss the miracle of experiencing the power of God to create His gifts in their hearts? Why would anyone resist His goodness? First, there is a war going on in our hearts, a war between our self-centered thinking and Jesus' love. When we experience the power of His goodness in our hearts, it leads us to understand more about our selfishness. So one reason we can miss the real meaning as we read His Word is that our self-centered thinking likes to protect itself and does not give up easily. We do not like to see ourselves as we really are, yet that is what will happen when we welcome the gifts He provides.

Another reason that we fail to experience His gifts and thus do not learn about His message of goodness in His Word is that we have not been convinced that Jesus always wants what is best for us. Even when things do not go the way we hoped, Jesus is on our side. While He is on our side, there are people we will encounter who are not. Jesus is all-powerful, yet He will not force people to do the right thing as though they are robots.

Since people can do the wrong thing, even horribly bad things, sometimes we suffer because of injustices, prejudices, and bad choices that other people embrace. That does not mean Jesus does not want what is best for us. It means we live in a selfish world where Jesus will not control everyone like robots.

Accepting that Jesus wants what is best for us, yet knowing that we will not always experience the good things He wants for us in life, can be a great challenge for us. It can become a barrier in our hearts that will keep us from experiencing the power of His goodness and thus keep us from understanding His Word. If we do not believe that Jesus is love, that He is good, that He seeks to help us, then why would we ask for His help to trust in Him and experience the power of His goodness?

To understand that Jesus always wants what's best for us, that He is all-powerful, and yet also knowing that it's possible for people to interfere with His plans is a challenge. Often we come to believe that our all-powerful, all knowing Creator exists to make our life easy and keep all bad things from happening to us. When we are happy and things are going as we plan, we can be confident that God loves us. Yet, God needs a relationship with us that goes beyond following Him because of what we believe He should do for us.

We must realize this earth is not operating as He originally designed it. There is an enemy who seeks to lead us away from Jesus and attack people who follow Him. If we blame God for the bad things that happen to us, or become disappointed because our expectations are not met, we will not embrace His goodness. If we want to understand the answers He yearns to give us, we must realize that we need to ask Him to help us trust in Him, to know that He always wants what is best for us.

To get answers to our deepest questions we must ask for His help to accept the fact that Jesus always loves us to the max. He wants what is best for us. That means what we ask for as we pray should not become an expectation. We should not begin to think, "If Jesus loves me, then He will do this for me." Jesus does not have to prove His love to us over and over through the things we want Him to do for us. So, if we pray for that new job that we really want, and it falls through, Jesus still loves us. If the cancer treatments are not producing the results we had hoped for, Jesus still loves us to the maximum. If we get in a car accident, make a bad investment, have our car stolen, or get fired, Jesus still loves us.

It is also true that, at times, Jesus will perform miracles on our behalf to make the best option a reality in our lives. He can interrupt the plans of those who seek to harm us or who seek to nullify His plans. God really did close the mouths of the lions when the prophet Daniel was thrown into the lions' den (see Daniel chapter 6). We also know that John the Baptist was not delivered from prison. He died. Yet, if Jesus had asked John the Baptist the question, "Would you rather be a witness of my goodness to King Herod and die because of it, or be silent to King Herod, keeping my goodness to yourself and live?" I believe John the Baptist would have agreed that the best option was to share the goodness of God with King Herod.

Jesus wants the best option for us, although even the best option can include suffering. We also need to realize that, because we live in a world that does not operate as Jesus originally designed, sometimes the best option does not happen. We need to be open to Plan B or even Plan C. Our relationship with Jesus cannot be a "what-have-you-done-for-me-lately" relationship. When Jesus creates His goodness, His love in our hearts, the good or bad events in our lives do not lead us to accept or doubt Jesus' love for us.

If we fail to accept the goodness Jesus seeks to create in our hearts because we do not think that He always wants the best option for us, we won't live with Him as our bread of life. We will be disappointed because He will never meet our expectations of what we believe He should do for us.

Living with Jesus as the bread of life means that He has convinced us that He wants what is best for us. That means as we ask Him to help us trust in Him, we can welcome the gifts He provides that show us what He is really like and what we are really like. Then He can perform the miracle of creating His goodness in our hearts. In doing so, we can understand His message in His Word, and thus gain insights to the answers He provides to the deepest questions we have in life.

No one can interfere with or take away from you the love, acceptance, and peace Jesus seeks to give you each day. Furthermore, if we fail to receive His gifts so we can understand His goodness as we read His Word, we will be confused by the answers He seeks to provide to the questions we ask. We might even become bitter toward Jesus as we become overwhelmed by what we perceive as a lack of answers.

CHAPTER EIGHT

More about Understanding His Goodness

To understand the answers Jesus provides to our questions in life we need to welcome the goodness He creates in our hearts, even though His gifts will challenge our entrenched self-centered way of thinking. In the last chapter, I explained the importance of allowing Jesus to create His goodness in our hearts so we can embrace the reality of His goodness. I also discussed how we need to be convinced that He loves and wants what is best for us, or we won't be committed to asking Him to create His goodness in our hearts.

Another crucial issue to embrace that will help us understand how Jesus answers our deepest questions with His goodness is to ask for His help to remember what He has taught us as we have studied the Bible. This seems like a simple issue, and yet I have found that, while many Christians read the Bible, few know how to study the Bible. To learn from the Bible as we study, we need to identify the solutions Jesus presents to the problems addressed in the passages we read. Then, Jesus will help us apply those solutions to our own lives.

Jesus' conversation with a group of religious leaders reveals that, if we want to understand His message of goodness, we need to understand how to read the Bible to grasp His solutions. The encounter began when Jesus saw an invalid, who had been sick for thirty-eight years, lying by the pool of Bethesda. Jesus asked him if He wanted to get well. He gave a hopeless answer about not being able to get into the pool of water before anyone else. The pool of Bethesda was connected with an urban legend. The legend said that, if you sat beside the water, waiting until you saw a ripple across the top of the water—the so-called "stirring of the waters," (John 5:4) that, if you went into the water first, you would be healed. What an empty legend that revealed the people's misguided perception of God!

Jesus looked at the invalid and told him something unexpected, "'…Get up! Pick up your mat and walk.' At once the man was cured; he picked up his mat and walked. The day on which this took place was a Sabbath" (John 5:8–9). Because Jesus healed someone on the Sabbath, it set up a conflict with the group of religious leaders. In fact, it led them to persecute Jesus and even seek to kill Him.

Jesus told the leaders that, while they sought to be very religious by studying the Scriptures, the Scriptures reveal Jesus' way of thinking, and they were rejecting Jesus' way of thinking. Jesus said, "You study the Scriptures diligently because you think that in them you have eternal life. These are the very Scriptures that testify about me, yet you refuse to come to me to have life. I do not accept glory from human beings, but I know you. I know that you do not have the love of God in your hearts" (John 5:39–42).

Jesus identified the problem with these religious leaders. They did not understand Jesus' actions because they did not understand God's goodness. In all that Jesus did, He revealed God's love. Yet, these religious leaders did not accept the works that He did as being from God, such as healing an invalid on the Sabbath who had been sick for thirty-eight years.

More about Understanding His Goodness ◆ 59

These religious leaders had a problem with understanding God's goodness. What solution did Jesus present to them? They needed a new way of studying the Scriptures that revealed Jesus' love. They had a good knowledge about the events in the Old Testament; however, they did not understand the message based on His goodness. That created a big problem. If they did not understand His goodness, how could they understand Jesus' answers to their questions when the answers He provided were based on His goodness?

They knew about Abraham, Moses, and Noah, but they did not know the message God wanted to give through these people. In other words, they failed to understand God's love, so they had a hard time accepting Jesus as He acted upon His goodness.

These religious leaders failed to understand how to study the Scriptures so that they could learn about God's love. Instead, they wanted to keep God at a distance and just focus on doing the right thing. They had no interest in learning from God about why His way of thinking was better than theirs. They had not experienced Him as the all-powerful Creator who could create goodness in their hearts.

Without an understanding of Jesus' goodness in His Word, these religious leaders became offended when He healed someone on the Sabbath. They tried to hide their inability to understand the Bible by focusing on an abundance of rules for keeping the Sabbath and for daily life.

Jesus tried to help these religious leaders understand their faulty thinking when He told them, "If you believed Moses, you would believe me, for he wrote about me. But since you do not believe what he wrote, how are you going to believe what I say?" (John 5:46, 47). These religious leaders needed a new way to study the Scriptures.

To read the Bible and understand God's love, His goodness, we need to ask Jesus for His help to trust in Him. Then He provides the gifts (love, joy, peace, patience, kindness, gentleness, goodness, etc.) that we need to understand Him as we read the Bible. What these religious leaders failed to understand is that the Scriptures present God's solutions to problems created by our human selfishness. In other words, the Bible is a book of solutions and should be studied that way.

With Jesus' help, we can understand the problem and the solution in passages as we read. As we identify the problem and thus can understand the solution, we will gain wonderful insights into His plan for our lives. Then as we compare and combine the solutions presented in Bible passages, we can clearly understand topics in the Bible. To get the most out of our Bible study we need to look for the problem in the passage, identify the solution, then compare and combine the solutions in the different stories and passages of the Bible—all of which is possible only with God's help and blessing.

It's interesting to take this conflict between Jesus and the religious leaders and compare it to and combine the solutions with those found in the next stories of the book of John—the feeding of the five thousand, followed by Jesus walking on the water. Remember, the problem with the religious leaders was that they did not know how to study the Word of God to see Jesus' love. They failed to understand the problems and God's solutions in His Word.

To clearly identify the problem and solution in a passage, we need to remember that the people God used to write the Bible expressed their ideas and experiences with God in their own words. God did not dictate the words of the Bible to them. The Holy Spirit inspired their thoughts and experiences; then they described their thoughts and experiences in their own words. This is why we are to let the entire Bible define and describe its terms and what it teaches. Therefore, we need to study the Bible by comparing and combining verses in their context and let the Bible develop a clear picture of the problem and God's solution based on His goodness. The religious leaders confronting Jesus did not understand this simple truth.

It is interesting to see how the next two stories in John reveal an insight into Jesus' encounter with these religious leaders. Remember the book of John was a letter that John wrote. Just as when we write down our thoughts in a letter, John had main points he sought to present. There is a flow of thought that develops and supports the points He wanted to make. With that in mind, it's interesting to see what stories John chose to include next.

At the end of chapter five, John wrote about how Jesus told the religious leaders that they may know the *stories* about Moses, but they did not understand the *message* of Moses. Now we need to compare and combine the story about Jesus and the religious leaders at the end of John chapter five with the next two stories in the beginning of John chapter six.

The first story in John chapter six is about Jesus feeding over five thousand people with five loaves and two fish. The problem in this passage was a simple one: the people following Jesus need to eat. Yet there was not enough food in this remote location to provide for all the people. What was Jesus' solution to the problem? Jesus revealed that He is the One Who will provide. Jesus took what His disciples thought was inadequate, five loaves and two fish, and created more loaves and fish to feed all the people. Now we can apply Jesus' solution to our lives today. Have you ever felt inadequate while witnessing to people, trying to share what you believe with others? Jesus can take those of us who feel inadequate and provide what we need so He can use us to "feed" others spiritually.

Does the Bible also have a story that happened to Moses about God solving a problem with feeding people through a miracle? Yes, as we looked at in the previous chapter, Moses led the people of Israel through the wilderness after their miraculous escape from Egypt. God's people faced a dire situation, a big problem, how could they get enough food to eat? God took an impossible situation (getting enough food for those who left Egypt) and provided the solution for them through His unlimited power. Each morning they would find small round pellets all over the ground; they called it *manna*. They gathered up the pellets that tasted like wafers made with honey and used them for food.

John included a story about how Jesus fed people in a miraculous way after Jesus told the religious leaders, "For if you believed Moses, you would believe me…" (John 5:46, NKJV). I believe John included the story about the feeding of the five thousand to help people make a connection with the story of the manna in the wilderness. God solved the problem with having food for the people in the wilderness, in the same way that Jesus solved the problem of not having enough food to feed all the people who followed Him. God's solution in these stories reveal that He seeks to be our provider. Because He is our all-powerful, loving Creator, He can provide for us in ways that seem impossible.

Next in the book of John comes the story about Jesus walking on the water. Does the Bible have a story about water that is associated with Moses? Yes, it does—the parting of the Red Sea. In the Red Sea story, the Egyptian army were chasing God's people after He miraculously delivered them from Egypt by means of the ten plagues. The Egyptians sought to capture God's people and bring them back to Egypt. God parted the Red Sea as the solution to the problem of being chased by the Egyptians.

The solution revealed an interesting fact. The solution to the Egyptian army problem came from the fact that God had chosen the descendants of Abraham, Isaac and Jacob to be His special people. God had a purpose, a mission for His special people to accomplish and He would lead them and protect them so that they could accomplish that mission.

The story about Jesus walking on the water also reveals that Jesus has a purpose, a mission for His special people to accomplish and He will lead them. Jesus walked on the water to the disciples as they encountered a storm with fierce winds that caused waves to crash against the side of their boat. The storm hindered the disciple's progress with what Jesus had asked them to do (see Mark 6:45). So, Jesus walked on the water to the boat, got into the boat, and the water calmed. Then the Bible says, "... immediately the boat reached the shore where they were heading" (John 6:21).

Just as Jesus walked on water to the disciples and helped them escape the storm so they could continue on their mission, God parted the Red Sea to enable His people to continue on the mission He had prepared for them. God parting the Red Sea and Jesus walking on the sea were both solutions to problems that hindered His people from accomplishing their mission.

If we want to follow the journey Jesus has for us as believers, choosing to follow Jesus' answers to the issues, conflicts, and challenges we face, then we cannot live as the religious leaders did, who failed to understand God's goodness as they studied the Bible. They misunderstood the stories about Moses because, first of all, they did not seek to let Jesus create His promises of love in their hearts as they read the Bible, as mentioned in the last chapter. Furthermore, they did not understand how the Scriptures reveal God's solutions to human problems.

In order to embrace the message of goodness that Jesus has for us in His Word, we must understand the solution to the problem mentioned in the passage, then compare and combine the solutions to get the full view of what is being taught on a subject. For example, Jesus feeding the people reveals that God is our provider and the story of Jesus walking on the water reveals that He will guide us as we follow His plans for helping others. Putting this all together means the religious leaders did not embrace Jesus as their provider or accept the mission of helping others understand more about God. As we understand the full view, we can apply what we learn to help us understand the answers He seeks to give us regarding the challenges and issues we face.

> *Do not look at the Bible as a collection of unrelated stories but as an unfolding message that uses the drama of real life to proclaim a message about God's goodness.*

We need to remember that the Old Testament informs the New Testament, and both describe the same eternal God of love. The Gospel of John as well as the other books of the Bible are not a collection of unrelated stories that just happen to be together. To understand the power of God's love in the stories of John, we need to understand the problem in the passage—God's solution to the problem in the passage—and then compare and combine the solutions together that we find in other passages—finding themes, similarities, and differences. Then we will not look at the Bible as a collection of unrelated stories, but as an unfolding message that uses the drama of real life to proclaim a message about God's goodness.

When we read the Bible by seeking to compare and combine together the solutions presented in the passages, we should use a both/and approach instead of an either/or perspective. The Bible is not a book of either/or rules. For example, either we obey or we are lost. That either/or perspective is not accurate because we can obey for the wrong reason and still be lost. The Bible uses both/and reasoning. Both law and grace go together; both mercy and judgment go together.

As you intentionally compare and combine the solutions presented in verses, chapters, and themes throughout the Bible, you will come to realize how the pieces fit together to give us an awesome, three-dimensional understanding of the Bible. Topics in the Bible are presented as a three-dimensional sculpture, not a flat painting. When looking at a sculpture, you have to walk around the sculpture to embrace its real beauty. In the same way, the great topics of the Bible do not work in isolation, they work together. Law, grace, mercy, and judgment all go together to enable us to understand the topic of salvation.

The gifts Jesus provides help us to embrace His goodness and trust in Him, which leads us to discover solutions in His Word that enable us to see Bible topics in three dimensions (3D). This 3D thinking means that we seek to look at Bible topics and challenges we face from difference perspectives, knowing that our self-centered way of thinking will try to blind us from seeing the full, amazing view of God's love.

Chapter Nine

Embracing Goodness

If you would like to understand how Jesus answers your questions with His goodness you can begin to incorporate the following routine into your daily prayer life. The routine works like this: put your issue or challenge into a question as you pray. For example, you can ask, "Why do I feel so lonely all the time?" or "How can I control my anger?" Next, let Him know why you ask this question. For example, "I am asking you to help me understand my loneliness because I do not have any good friends."

Next, ask Jesus, "Please help me to understand Your answer to my question." That means you will need to ask Him for help to embrace His goodness. You will need to ask Him to help you embrace His goodness in three specific ways. First, ask Jesus to help you trust that He desires the best option for you with the issue or challenge you face. He will work on your behalf even though the best option might include suffering. He can intervene on your behalf, to open a door for the best option. Also understand that, since He does not force other people who might be involved in the issue to follow His ways, He has a Plan B and a Plan C.

Second, ask Him to help you by creating His goodness in your heart. As your all-powerful Creator, He desires to give you the gifts of peace, joy, compassion, comfort, and much more each day in your soul. He provides these gifts to sooth your anxiety or fears. These gifts will give your mind the opportunity to relax, to find relief from any stress, and to be open to what He seeks to help you understand.

Third, ask Jesus to help you remember what He has taught you in the past about His goodness in His Word. For example, Jesus may remind you that He wants to be your provider, as seen in the stories about the manna in the desert and the feeding of the five thousand. As you ask Him to help you remember the solutions He has revealed based on His goodness, He can bring Bible verses and experiences to your mind to illustrate His way of thinking and why it is always the best way. He will help you remember how His love, joy, peace, patience, kindness, gentleness, forgiveness, mercy, grace, and wisdom have worked in your life, the lives of others, and in stories in the Bible.

As you ask Him to help you embrace His goodness, He can give you insights into how His goodness applies to your issue, challenge, or situation. But then, to understand His answer, you need to be aware of a glaring misconception in the Christian world today—that most often He won't answer you by telling you what to do. At the same time, He also won't dismiss you and leave you without a next step to take. He seeks to help you understand more about yourself and His way of thinking, not just to tell you what to do. He will challenge your priorities, what you value, and any prejudices you have and what you cherish most, but He always does this with love.

He will provide you with assurance of His commitment to you—that He loves you and has an awesome plan for your life! His first priority is to help you apply His way of thinking to your question. He will help you understand how His goodness guides the answers He gives you. That means you need to be willing, to not get a direct answer to your question but instead to continue to seek to understand how His goodness applies to your issue.

To get a better idea of how to understand His answers to your questions, here are some examples. If you found yourself in a position where you really hoped to get a new job, you might ask Jesus, "Will I get that new job I seek?" Next, let Him know why you are asking this question. You might say, "I seek this new job because of the increase in pay, and I would like the challenge of the additional responsibility."

> *You get your sense of value and worth from Jesus, not from a job... Jobs come and go, but a relationship with Jesus should be the enduring constant in our lives.*

Then ask Jesus to help you understand His answer by helping you embrace His goodness in three specific ways. First, ask Jesus, "Help me to trust that You will lead me to or give me the best answer." Second, "Help me understand by creating your goodness in my heart right now." Third, "Help me to remember what you have taught me about Your goodness in Your Word."

Now you are ready to embrace the answer He provides. Instead of just looking for an answer that tells you what to do or dismisses your need to cooperate with Him, He will help you embrace an answer that reveals His goodness. It might be that, in asking a question such as, "Will I get that new job?" Jesus would lead you to remember that He has promised in His Word to provide for you and your family. Then He might have you recall how, over and over in so many ways, He has shown you that His promise is real. He can also provide the gifts you need at this time, like creating peace and assurance in your soul that will help you to trust Him with the unknown, so that you can be confident that He wants the best option for you and others, such as your family.

With His goodness in your mind and heart, the answer to your question might become one of helping you with your job expectations. Have you taken everything about this new job into consideration? Jesus might lead you to contemplate whether you have turned this new job opportunity into a statement about your self-worth. Jesus empowers you to have value in His sight with whatever job you have. Wherever you work, Jesus wants you to put Him first. You get your sense of value and worth from Jesus, not from a job.

We should remember that, with every question we ask Jesus, He wants us to learn more about His goodness and about ourselves. A relationship with Jesus does not mean He will always reveal what will happen in the future, for example whether we will get a job or not. But we know we can trust Him with our future. Jobs come and go, but a relationship with Jesus should be the enduring constant in our lives.

Jesus will give you an answer that reflects His goodness and helps you understand more about yourself. Now, you can believe the answer He gave you by choosing to follow His answer. So you pray, "Thank you, Jesus, for answering my question. I choose to derive my self-worth, my value, from You. You bring the healing of forgiveness and the peace I need to my soul. Thank you for these gifts. Thank you for helping me to remember what you what taught me in Your Word about being my provider. I ask for your help to accept you as my provider each day, with respect to both my job and my self-worth." Then, ask Jesus to help you follow the commitment you made to His answer.

Consider another example. If you ask Jesus, "Why do I feel so lonely all the time?" Then tell Him why you are asking Him this question. Next, ask Jesus to please help you to understand His answer to your question by helping you embrace His goodness in three specific ways.

First, ask Him to help you understand the answer He seeks to give you, by asking Him, "Help me to trust in you, that you will help me with the best option. I know you can intervene on my behalf to open a door for the best option. I also know that sometimes people can interfere with your plans and that the best option can include suffering."

Second, ask Jesus, "Help me by creating the gifts of your goodness in my heart." Let Jesus provide the gifts of assurance, peace, and joy in your soul right now. With His peace in your heart, you can more easily discern how His goodness can help you.

Third, ask Him to help you remember what He has taught you about His solutions to problems in the past—solutions that revealed His goodness in His Word. He might answer you by bringing to mind a Bible verse, such as the verse that says, "But if we walk in the light, as he is in the light, we have fellowship with one another…" (1 John 1:7). This verse reveals how real friendship develops by walking in the light.

Now you are ready to embrace the answer He provides which reveals His goodness and does not just tell you what to do or dismiss your need to cooperate with Him. As Jesus helped you remember 1 John 1:7, He can help you discover how walking in the light leads to positive friendship with others and that walking in the light comes first. So, in this example, instead of focusing on how to not be lonely, or waiting for Jesus to give you a to-do list for how to make friends, He will lead you to focus on walking in the light with Him each day.

Next, you need to let Jesus know that you believe His answer, that you choose to follow the answer He has provided about feeling lonely. Pray and let Him know this by saying, "I choose to walk in the light with You each day. I realize that walking in the light comes first. It will lead to friendships with others, which can lead me away from loneliness." Then you will need to ask Him for his help to keep the commitment you just made. Of course, that should lead to another question you can ask Jesus, "What does it mean to walk in the light?" Then you start the process over again. In this way, you can receive real answers to your questions that go beyond just telling you what to do. He can empower you to live with His goodness in your heart.

Jesus does not seek to answer the question, "Why do I feel so lonely all the time?" with a direct answer like, "Go make some friends" or "If you would go to church more, you might have more friends." He leads us to the answer by helping us understand, experience, and believe in His goodness. Please understand that this hypothetical answer does not apply to all people who experience loneliness. It is just an example of how He might answer one person. Jesus will answer in a way that addresses the solution He has for you, as someone with unique needs. Jesus will often give different answers to people who ask Him the same question. He will answer each of us according to what He knows we need.

Jesus seeks to answer your questions from the perspective of His goodness. He will remind you of what He has taught you about His character, His goodness, and why His way of thinking is better. Then, with His power, He can create goodness in your heart by providing real gifts to relieve your fears. Then, as He helps you to trust that He always wants the best option for you, you can discern how His goodness applies to the issues, challenges, and situations you ask Him about.

Please do not fall into the trap of thinking that Jesus always leads you by telling you what to *do*, or that you think that you have nothing to do or learn. He leads you to choose His goodness. A relationship with Him is much, much more exciting than just seeking to do the right thing or thinking His grace dismisses your need to cooperate with Him.

Chapter Ten

Doing the Right Thing

Can living as a non-Christian be more attractive than living as a Christian? Yes, unfortunately, some people can portray it that way. Yet, if you believe living as a non-Christian is more appealing than living as a Christian, please consider that you misunderstand something about Christianity.

As I shared earlier in this book, I didn't read John 3:16 in a Bible until I was twenty-seven years old. I enjoyed traveling down the road of life with a big chocolate donut in one hand and a large coffee in the other, driving with my knees. And, as a proud American male, I would not even think about stopping to ask anyone for directions. I lived my life my way. I could go out and party late into the night, sleep in, go to work, and go out the next night—no problem. It did not bother me at all; I slept just fine. I focused on how much fun I could have (my definition of "fun"). I only worried about how successful I could become, not the damage I did to other people with my choices. Then, after becoming a Christian, the things I did began to bother me. Before, as a non-Christian, I did what I wanted when I wanted. As a Christian, that all changed.

In becoming a Christian, I had gained something new, something I did not have in my life before. I gained a definition for *goodness*. For the first time, I could understand goodness and why Jesus always promoted goodness. I began to strive to make choices based on Jesus' definition of *goodness*. I wanted to learn about His way of living. I welcomed the conviction, correction, forgiveness, and strength He offered me.

Forgiveness did not have a place in my life before letting Jesus define His goodness. As I learned about how He defined goodness, it led me to ask for His forgiveness for my poor choices. To my amazement, His forgiveness empowered better choices. However, I found that my selfishness could put a nasty twist even in my relationship with Jesus.

> *However, by focusing on doing the "right thing" instead of asking for Jesus' help to be honest about my desires, I found myself trying to do the right thing without His help.*

As time passed, I began to develop a strong desire to "do what was right." That way I could live a life that honored God. I had done the wrong thing so often that I became driven to do the right thing. It seemed like a good thing to ask, "Jesus, please help me to do the right thing." However, I encountered a big problem with this perspective.

Wanting to do the right thing seemed like a great way to live. Yet, I discovered that it led me to focus on my behavior, and that became a problem. By focusing on my behavior, I found it easier to get sidetracked into thinking, *If I just do the right thing, then things will work out for me.* I developed a selfish motive for wanting to do the right thing. I started to think of my relationship with Jesus as a way to get what I wanted.

I began to think that if I can just do the right thing, then I will be safe and blessed by Jesus. However, by focusing on doing the "right thing" instead of asking for Jesus' help to be honest about my desires, I found myself trying to do the right thing without His help. His correction became something I did not need. I did not spend time with Jesus asking Him to search my heart. It made me feel better about myself if He did not correct me. It felt like I was improving, doing more of the right thing. Yet, in reality, I began to ignore Jesus.

So, early in my walk with Jesus, wanting to do the right thing became a trap. When things did not work out the way I wanted, I thought I needed to get better at *doing* the right thing. This, in turn, made me less tolerant of others who were not doing the right thing as I was trying to do. When good things happened to people who did not do the right thing, I became confused and a little annoyed. *Why do things work out for them when they are not doing the right thing?* I would ask myself.

This led me to focus more on the religious things that I did well, things that came easily to me. In that way, my behavior began to provide the positive feedback my selfishness craved. I could take comfort that I was all right with Jesus because of the things I did. In fact, I could make a list of the right things I did well. To me, at that time, the Ten Commandments seemed to be a good list to start with—do not lie, do not steal, no adultery, etc. Then I added, do not use cuss words, do not eat unhealthy foods, do not drink caffeine, do not drink alcohol, do not read novels, do not…do not—you get the idea. That is not a bad list of things to avoid. However, I found it easier to have a list of "don'ts" that led me to do the right thing than inviting Jesus to search my heart and so He could teach me about His goodness.

Because of my "do-the-right-thing" commitment, I began to be less tolerant of others. In other words, focusing on doing the right thing did not make me more loving. I became less loving toward others, and I had less empathy. However, should a relationship with Jesus make us *less* loving toward other people? I needed to ask myself that question.

Early in my relationship with Jesus, I failed to understand that Jesus did not design the plan of salvation as a competition to be won or lost. I created a real problem for myself by focusing on my behavior. I thought that everything would work out great for me in life if I just did my part by doing the right things.

Yet, you might ask, isn't behavior important? Don't our choices matter? Yes, Jesus does hold us accountable for our actions. He is our Judge. However, we need a relationship with Jesus that allows the Holy Spirit to get at the heart of the problem—our desires. Our behavior is the result of our desires. We can even do the right thing for the wrong reason. If we focus on our behavior, bypassing our need to be transformed with new desires, then we will try to "fake it" with our behavior. Then, looking to our behavior as evidence for our salvation can become a big problem.

When we focus on our behavior, we miss the reality described in Titus 3:5, 6 that tells us, "…not by works of righteousness which we have done, but according to His mercy He saved us, through the washing of regeneration and renewing of the Holy Spirit, whom He poured out on us abundantly through Jesus Christ our Savior…" (NKJV). The washing and regeneration presented in these verses is that of our desires. Jesus seeks to help us have new desires that come from His definition of goodness. That is what it means to learn from Jesus, as He answers our questions from His goodness perspective. His goodness will cleanse our desires and renew our hearts, helping us to understand why His way is better. Romans 2:4 says that the goodness of God leads us to repentance.

When we let the Holy Spirit search and test our hearts, as King David wrote—"Search me, O God, and know my heart…and see if there is any wicked way in me…(Ps. 139: 23, 24), then Jesus can help us understand more about His way of thinking, and that should make us rejoice! It is the goodness of God, His goodness, which leads us to repentance. It is that process of regenerating, redesigning, reprioritizing, and recreating our desires, that, in turn, guides our choices and thus impacts behavior.

Jesus seeks to help us embrace His goodness, yet Jesus does much, much more than just teach us about His goodness. Because Jesus is our all-powerful Creator, He can supernaturally create His goodness in our hearts. He creates the gifts of joy in our hearts that lead us to worship Him; He creates kindness toward others that leads us to tell the truth instead of a lie; and He creates empathy and compassion for men and women involved in pornography, leading us to pray for them because they believe that they have no other value or purpose in life. He puts contentment in our hearts that enables us to be happy with what we have. He gives us assurance that He accepts us when we make mistakes. The list of His provisions goes on and on. So, that means we don't choose between lying or not, stealing or not, having an affair or not. We choose Jesus' goodness instead of lying, His goodness instead of stealing, His goodness instead of having an affair. So, our behavior is the fruit that grows naturally from dependence on and cooperation with Jesus, not from a strong will that just focuses on doing the right thing.

We have the privilege of embracing a relationship with an all-powerful Creator who can teach us about His goodness, help us to experience His goodness, and help us to trust that He always wants the best option for us. We sell ourselves short if we only have a "do-the-right-thing" relationship with Jesus.

Remember the religious leaders who persecuted Jesus for healing a man on the Sabbath who had been sick for thirty-eight years? Jesus told them, "but I know you. I know that you do not have the love of God in your hearts" (John 5:42). Jesus got the same kind of reaction after He raised a man named Lazarus from the dead. In describing the reaction of the religious leaders to the raising of Lazarus, the Bible says, "So from that day on they plotted to take his [Jesus'] life" (John 11:53).

Focusing on doing the right thing misses the point. It leads us to an empty place—relying on our own will power. The real issue is not behavior. We need new desires. As we invite Jesus to lead us each day, He gives us new desires that lead to choices that improve our lives. All of our righteousness is as filthy rags, worthless. We cannot earn merit with God for the things we do because that is impossible; instead, we are given what is called *grace*.

I would like to also note the opposite deception to "doing the right thing," and that is the falsehood that grace excuses us from our need to cooperate with Jesus. This is the thought that, because of grace, what we do does not matter. Any road we travel has these ditches on each side. We can get off the road by focusing on "doing the right thing" but also get off the road by thinking that what we do does not matter.

To keep on the road with Jesus as a believer, we need His help each day to trust in Him; we need to invite Him to search our hearts, and then we need to make a conscious choice to embrace His goodness. Remember, faith does not mean that, if we become convinced something should happen, it will happen. Faith is trust, yet we need Jesus' help to trust in Him. Faith leads us to ask for Jesus' help to trust in His way of thinking more and more each day. As we trust in Him more, we will grow in our relationship with Him and become committed to first asking Him questions about the challenges, situations, and issues we face.

Jesus will answer us the only way He can, with His goodness. We have the privilege of seeking His goodness each day. Don't go down that path of trying to just do the right thing. Ask Jesus questions; He will answer! Jesus can help us discover the next step to take, based on an understanding of how His goodness applies to our question.

Learning about His goodness represents a miraculous part of our relationship with Jesus. The Holy Spirit will tutor us to help us understand His goodness in the Bible and then help us apply it to our lives. Because Jesus is all powerful, He can create the gifts of His goodness in our hearts and minds. Just as He created light and substance, He can create joy, peace, patience, gentleness, kindness, and self-control in our souls. So, we do not just intellectually understand His goodness, but the Holy Spirit explains His goodness to us each day and we can *experience* His goodness in our hearts and minds.

To accept His goodness means we realize that Jesus wants to do what's best for us, yet we also understand that not all people want what is best for us. Jesus cannot force people to follow Him, so that means we can suffer from the choices of people who do not know Jesus and from the choices of people who want to follow Jesus but do not understand how to let His goodness lead with their choices.

While Jesus cannot force people to follow His goodness, He does, at times, intervene to override the wrong choices of others that affect us. God really did shut the mouths of the lions when the prophet Daniel was thrown into the lions' den (Dan. 6:22). And yet, after John the Baptist was arrested, Jesus did not deliver Him from prison. Tragedies happen; things that make Jesus sad happen every day. At the same time, Jesus always has a best option for us.

Choosing to follow the answers that Jesus provides means we live as a believer. To believe means to choose, to make a commitment to follow the answers He provides. Having faith means to trust, yet we need to reach out to Jesus for help to trust in Him with the questions we ask. He will provide the gifts that we need to understand His answers to our questions. Believing means we accept (choose) the answer He provides. After choosing to follow His answer, we need to ask for His help to keep the commitment we have made to His answer. We cannot keep the commitments we make to those answers without His help.

Chapter Eleven
Getting Answers

Atheists believe in evolution; Christians believe in a Creator. Hindus have a different set of beliefs and Buddhists another. Then, within Christianity, there are Baptist, Methodist, Seventh-day Adventist, Presbyterian, Church of God, Episcopal, Lutheran, Catholic, and non-denominational churches—all of which have different beliefs and teachings. They all claim to have the answers from God, yet can these contradictory teachings all be true?

All of these truths have competing ideas. They each contain elements that contradict each other, so they cannot all be true. Atheists and Christians cannot both be correct. So how can we get answers in which we can trust?

Consider a question that the Roman Governor (Pontius Pilate) asked after Jesus told him that "everyone on the side of truth listens to me" (John 18:37). Pilate responded by saying, "What is truth?" As with many people today, the Roman Governor had been exposed to so many different teachers of truth that he had lost interest in seeking truth. With so many different truths, isn't one truth just as good as another?

How can we know what is true or real today? If you have been a Christian for many years and have not received answers to your questions, here is your opportunity. If Christianity is something that you are exploring, here is your chance to find truth. You can ask your Creator questions, and you can get answers. Try it out for yourself and see that it is true. To help you understand more about this process of getting answers to your questions from your Creator, the rest of this chapter will provide hypothetical examples of people who have gotten answers.

Let's say that a man named John had a boss at work who gave him a hard time he did not deserve. John has tried to follow the suggestions his boss has made, yet the suggestions continue to multiply. John talked about this issue with his boss, yet things only became worse. He has noticed how His boss treats other people with the same critical attitude. John has been praying about the situation, but it still bothers him greatly, He can't sleep well at night, and he would really like to get help. The job pays well and he likes the work, but his boss continues to be a problem.

> *He realized there's nothing Jesus can lead him to do that will force his boss to change. Jesus can lead John to witness to his boss, yet it's his boss's choice to change.*

John decided to put the issue he faced into the following question to ask Jesus: "Jesus, why does my boss give me a hard time?" As he made this question an issue of prayer, he told Jesus he asked this question because he would like to keep his job. John then asked Jesus for His help to understand His answer. Since John knew that Jesus would answer him from His goodness perspective, he asked for Jesus' help to trust that He will provide the best option, even though people can interfere with "Plan A" and the best option can include suffering. John asked

Jesus to help him by creating His goodness, His gifts—His love, joy, peace, patience, kindness, and gentleness in his heart. He also asked Jesus for help in remembering the things he had learned about His goodness in His Word.

Jesus helped John to realize that He can't change his boss unless his boss would like to be changed. Jesus won't change people who do not seek His help. He realized there's nothing Jesus can lead him to do that will force his boss to change. Jesus can lead John to witness to his boss, yet it's his boss's choice to change. John also realized that Jesus could give him peace that brings real relief from his boss' critical attitude each day.

Now John knew what to do. He asked Jesus for wisdom to know tactful ways to witness to His boss, and also for Jesus' help to let His goodness protect him from the critical attitude of his boss. John wrote down Jesus' answer to his question in this way: *As my boss continues to give me a hard time, I believe that each day Jesus will help me remember the abundant forgiveness He has given me and will fill my heart with His peace when I feel the stress that my boss creates in my heart. And when I fail, Jesus will remind me of His love and forgiveness.*

Instead of focusing on getting Jesus to change His boss, John has a real answer from Jesus based on His goodness. John now can focus on letting Jesus change his own perspective. Jesus' answer provided John with a next step to take. John decided that his next step would be to get up a little earlier each morning before going to work so he can spend time with Jesus in prayer and reading His Word, preparing himself to deal with his boss.

Just imagine how things might change at work. John has Jesus' goodness in his heart, with an attitude of forgiveness and peace. The rude comments don't penetrate his heart anymore. At times, His boss' comments might still get under his skin, yet John does not sit and repeat those comments over and over in his mind anymore. John can now encourage other employees who also have been wounded by the inconsiderate words of his boss. This is an example of how John's faith (asking for Jesus' help), was answered by Jesus' goodness, and led him to believe (choose to follow Jesus' answer).

Here's another hypothetical example from a couple named April and Joe; both are in their mid-thirties, and they have recently become Christians. Their lives as non-Christians left them a few difficult situations to resolve. The most difficult for them is the possibility of losing their home because April lost her job. The loss of her job led to problems paying their maxed-out credit cards and high mortgage payments. Each day they live with the dread of losing their home. April has applied for job after job but has not been hired. As weeks turn into months and the bank notice letters pile up and the stress increases, they wonder about their new faith.

They both feel guilty for the way they wasted their money before becoming Christians. They remember all the lavish trips and expensive dinners they put on their credit cards. Now they regret their past approach to managing money. At times, they wonder if Jesus will help them because they realize how they got themselves into this financial mess.

April and Joe became Christians because they saw the goodness of God working through one of Joe's co-workers. Joe could not understand why his co-worker, James, spent so much of his time helping with things at church. James helped with meals for the homeless, taught a class for teens, and spent time on the weekends painting rooms and maintaining the church. Whenever Joe asked James why he gave his time to do things at church when he could be out having fun, James just told Joe, "That *is* fun for me."

The fact that James actually thought giving away his time to the church was fun really got under Joe's skin. Until one day Joe told James, "I just do not get you. You call things fun that I would never call fun." Then James asked Joe, "Well, Joe, how about you and April come over for dinner on Wednesday evening? My wife Ellen will be there and we can talk about it." To James' surprise, Joe and April said, "Yes." Their conversation over dinner led to a Bible study, which led to more dinners, and more Bible studies. Over the next eight months, Joe and April began to understand more about Jesus' way of thinking, and they experienced the power of Jesus' goodness to create peace, joy, and kindness in their hearts. This led Joe and April to choose to be baptized at James and Ellen's church.

They had become trapped by debt from their previous lifestyle. Yet, because they saw the goodness of God working through James and Ellen's lives, as Joe and April began to seek an answer to their debt problem, they looked to Jesus' goodness. It inspired them to be baptized, to embrace a relationship with Him, and join the church. Now it seemed natural for them to seek Jesus' goodness in answer to their debt question.

They began to ask Jesus in prayer, "Would you please help us to keep our home?" They also told Jesus why they asked Him this question, and then asked Him, "Please help us understand Your answer to our question." Next, they asked Jesus to help them trust that He would provide the best option, even though people can interfere with Plan A and the best option might include suffering. Then they asked Him to create His goodness, His love, joy, peace, patience, kindness, goodness, gentleness, and self-control in their hearts. His gifts of goodness provided relief from stress and gave insights into His answer. Finally, they asked Jesus to help them remember what He has taught them about His goodness in His Word.

Joe and April asked others at church to pray for their debt situation. One day after church, a new friend named Sam asked if they had ever watched a seminar on Christian finances called Financial Peace University by Dave Ramsey. Sam and his wife invited them to come to their home for dinner and to watch one of those DVD presentations. After they watched the first DVD, Joe and April made a commitment to follow Jesus' plan for their finances. They understood His plan and why it was better. The next day, Sam sent Joe a text letting him know that he and his wife had purchased the Financial Peace University DVD set for them.

April and Joe got excited about what they learned, and for the first time they could see that God's goodness would lead them to manage their money wisely. They understood the risk of losing their home, and yet they also knew Jesus would be with them no matter what happened, even if they did lose their home. They next took the step of cutting up their credits cards, and they found a way to live on one income. It took time, and they had to make sacrifices, but, over the years, they became debt free and enjoyed the financial freedom that God brought into their lives.

In another example, Sarah and Rob have been married for over twenty years. They both grew up in Christian homes, yet they met in college during a time when they both had walked away from the church. It had been ten years since they had been to church, and the news they just received shook them to the core.

Sarah had been experiencing some shortness of breath. She also lost some weight recently. After visiting her doctor and completing several tests the doctor ordered, Sarah received the bad news that she had stage four lung cancer.

As anyone could understand, both Sarah and Rob struggled with the cancer diagnosis. They wondered if this was God's way of getting back at them for living a life that did not honor Him while in college. She had smoked cigarettes and pot, and had gotten drunk one or two nights a week for about eight years during that time in her life. Was God now punishing her?

Some people at church just made things worse. One friend told them that, if they had real faith, they would not even need any treatments from the doctors. Jesus would heal them if they just had faith. Other people at church said they would pray for them, and yet the situation did not change. Sarah kept getting worse, and the treatment plan did not seem to help with the cancer.

Then one day she read a book a friend had given her entitled, *Discover the Power of Goodness and Find Your Answers*. She had never thought about how Jesus sought to lead her with His goodness, even with her cancer. So, Sarah and Rob began to pray, "Jesus, would you please heal this cancer?" They also shared with Jesus why they asked this question and asked Him, "Please help us understand Your answer to our question."

Next, they asked Jesus to help them trust that He would provide the best option, even though people can interfere with "Plan A" and the best option can include suffering. Then they asked Him to help them by creating the gifts of His love, joy, peace, patience, kindness, goodness, gentleness, faithfulness, self-control, forgiveness, wisdom, and peace in their hearts, providing relief from their stress and insights into Jesus' answer. Finally, they asked Jesus to help them remember the solutions to problems He had showed them in His Word.

One day about a week later, as Rob went for a walk alone on a nature trail near their home, he began praying to Jesus and asking for His help to trust in Him. He had recently started studying the Bible in a new way, a way that helped Him understand the goodness of God. While walking and praying, he became impressed that he and Sarah had been looking at the cancer issue in the wrong way. It was not a punishment. It was not something Jesus brought into their lives. Rob was convicted that Jesus would help them, yet there was no guarantee of an outcome. Rob chose to embrace Jesus' goodness, no matter what happened. He became convinced that Jesus is always good and wants the best for them. Jesus helped Rob understand that the best response would be to take the battle against cancer one day at a time. Each day, with Jesus beside them, they could find ways, even small ways, to help Sarah in her fight with cancer. Yet, no matter what happened, Rob believed Jesus loved them and was committed to both of them.

Therefore, along with the prescribed chemotherapy drugs, they also found some herbs that could help to build up Sarah's immune system. They discovered how simple hydrotherapy treatments could help. Through the process of time, one day at a time, they found answers: a diet and other information that helped cancer patients. They made sure Sarah drank plenty of purified water, so they installed a reverse osmosis filtration system in their house. Each day they focused on Jesus' goodness, knowing that He would guide yet could not guarantee an outcome. It seemed like each day Jesus gave them new insights into her health and His love for them. The battle with cancer continued, with good days and bad days.

They experienced the goodness of God, even with a tragic cancer diagnosis. They did not have a guilty, beaten-down, hopeless perspective. As they studied the Bible together more often, their confidence in God grew. They believed that God would help Sarah, and yet, even if the cancer did take her life, they knew that God loved them both and the best (heaven and eternity) was yet to come.

So, what is truth? The answer is that you can find out for yourself. You do not have to take my word for it or someone else's word. You can get the answers to your questions from your Creator.

Chapter Twelve

Answers from His Word

Can everyone understand the Bible? Well, Jesus actually said, "No." Not everyone can understand the Bible. When did Jesus say this? Once after Jesus had been teaching His disciples, they asked Him, "…Why do You speak to them the people in parables?' He replied, 'Because the knowledge of the secrets of the kingdom of heaven has been given to you, but not to them. Whoever has will be given more, and they will have an abundance. Whoever does not have, even what they have will be taken from them. This is why I speak to them in parables: Though seeing, they do not see; though hearing, they do not hear or understand'" (Matt. 13:10–13). Jesus gave an interesting answer. It seems that understanding His Word would not be for everyone. To some, the knowledge of the kingdom of heaven would not be given, but why?

Does this passage in the Bible mean that some people cannot understand the secrets or mysteries of the kingdom of heaven? Well, yes and no. To some people, the kingdom of heaven is "foolishness" (1 Cor. 1:23). To understand the secrets or mysteries of the kingdom of heaven, people need to have a hunger or thirst to understand. Jesus does not deliberately withhold knowledge from some people and give it to others.

So, what makes the difference between people who understand and those who do not understand? Jesus described in more detail those who do not understand in verses 13–15 of Matthew 13. "Though seeing, they do not see; though hearing, they do not hear or understand…. For this people's heart has become calloused; they hardly hear with their ears, and they have closed their eyes. Otherwise, they might see with their eyes, hear with their ears, understand with their hearts and turn, and I would heal them."

To hear with our ears and not have our eyes closed, we need to ask for and receive help from Jesus to understand His Word. To have ears that hear and eyes that see means we seek His help to understand His goodness as we read His Word. We seek to understand what a verse or passage means, not just what it says.

For example, Jesus said, "But I tell you that everyone will have to give account on the day of judgment for every empty word they have spoken" (Matt. 12:36). If we take this verse just at what it says, then we could come to the conclusion that Jesus is harsh—that if you have spoken any "empty" or idle words in your past, you will not be going to heaven.

However, we should never read verses in the Bible in isolation. We need to pray and ask Jesus to help us understand His goodness and realize that to discover what is real in the Bible we need to find the solution to the problem in the passage and need to connect the solutions together like a sculpture with many parts. We must understand the problem presented and the solution offered in the passage and other related passages. The problem in Matthew 12:36 is that we will face a judgment from God that includes our words.

What is the solution to the problem in Matthew 12:36? If we include the verse before and the verse after Matthew 12:36, they say, "A good man brings good things out of the good stored up in him, and an evil man brings evil things out of the evil stored up in him. But I tell you that everyone will have to give account on the day of judgment for every empty word they have spoken. For by your words you will be acquitted, and by your words you will be condemned" (Matt. 12:35–37). The solution to the problem of facing a judgment that includes our own words is that our words can reveal His goodness. Luke 6:45 tell us, "A good man brings good things out of the good stored up in his heart, and an evil man brings forth evil things out of the evil stored up in his heart. For the mouth speaks what the heart is full of." Therefore, with Jesus' help, we can be acquitted; proven innocent by the words we speak out of the goodness He places in our hearts.

We need to then compare and combine verses to get an accurate picture of what the Bible teaches in Matthew 12:36. So, from Matthew 12:36 we can understand that there is a judgment that includes what we say as evidence, yet we can compare and combine that with Matthew 11:28–30 that tells us, "Come to me all you who are weary and burdened, and I will give you rest. Take my yoke upon you and learn from me, for I am gentle and humble in heart, and you will find rest for your souls. For my yoke is easy and my burden is light."

The problem in Matthew 11:28–30 is that we all have heavy burdens that make us weary. The solution is to learn from Jesus, about His goodness, and He will give us rest (a gift) that heals our weariness. Matthew 11:28–30 goes with Matthew 12:36. They both fit together to give us a view of Jesus' goodness and the judgment. Matthew 11:28–30 does not include the word *judgment*. Yet it is a description of the kind of relationship Jesus holds us accountable for. Therefore, it is a good example of how to study the Bible with a 360-degree perspective, putting the pieces together like a sculpture. We should understand that the judgment verses and the relationship with Jesus verses go together.

Jesus will hold us accountable, and yet His "yoke" (a farming term that describes a wooden crosspiece attached to necks of two animals that are used to pull a wagon or plow) is easy and His burden is light. Jesus does not seek to overwhelm our lives with harsh, rigid rules to make our burdens heavy. Jesus does not seek to be a harsh, task master Judge in our lives. He seeks to heal our weariness and inspire us to speak out of the goodness He provides.

When we seek to understand what the Bible means, not just what it says—by understanding the problem and the solution in the passage, then comparing and combining the solutions together we can learn more about Jesus' goodness. To embrace Jesus' goodness as the answer to your deepest questions in life, you will need to ask for His help to remember what He has taught you about His goodness in His Word. So that means the more you understand about His goodness in His Word, the more He can help you understand His answers to your questions.

In the previous chapter, I used a hypothetical example about seeking Jesus' goodness in dealing with a difficult boss at work. How might understanding His goodness from His Word empower someone who asked Jesus for His help in dealing with a difficult boss?

If someone wanted insights from the Bible about dealing with a difficult boss, they could compare and combine Luke 6:27, 28 with Romans 8:28 to have a healthy insight into that question. Luke 6:27, 28 says, "But to you who are listening I say: Love your enemies, do good to those who hate you, bless those who curse you, pray for those who mistreat you." In this passage, Jesus addressed the problem we face in trying to love those who mistreat us. The solution is that His love is powerful enough to help us love and pray for our enemies. Yet how can we do that? Romans 8:28 tells us, "And we know that in all things God works for the good of those who love him, who have been called according to his purpose." This verse reminds us that we all have issues and challenges in our lives that are confusing or unpleasant. The solution is to remember that God really is in control. While we may suffer and not get our way, in the end, all things will work to His favor as we follow Him. We can learn important lessons through the difficulties and trials we face, and God will use all those things to draw us closer to Him.

Putting Luke 6:27, 28 together with Romans 8:28 tells us that we can love and pray for those who mistreat us, those who act as enemies towards us, because we believe that all things work for good for those who love Jesus. God really is in control. We may suffer, endure disappointments and failures, and yet, in the end, we will understand how all things really did work to His good.

So, applying Jesus' goodness to the situation of a difficult boss means remembering that in all things God will work for the good of those who love Him. That means we believe Jesus is in control and, thus, we can even love and pray for those who mistreat us. We do not need to let a difficult boss steal our joy or confidence, even when God seems to be silent or we do not feel as if God is defending us. With Jesus in our hearts, we are not victims. He will use all things to draw us closer to Him and, in the end, Jesus (and those that follow Him) will win.

The second hypothetical example I used in the previous chapter told the story of Joe and April and the debt problem they faced. How might remembering what they had studied in the Bible help them understand Jesus' plan? In many stories, the Bible reveals that we can trust in Jesus as our provider. He will help Joe and April with their financial situation.

As they look at their problems and then compare and combine what the Bible teaches about Jesus being their provider in different passages, the Bible reveals that Jesus will help them find good jobs, avoid debt, and lead them to find happiness outside of monetary reward. They can trust Jesus with their future.

Joe and April can embrace the fact that Jesus delights in being their provider. They can understand why God informs them that ten percent of their increase in value belongs to Him. In fact, God is clear about what is called *a tithe*. *Tithe* means ten percent. God claims it as His. It does not belong to them. God asks them to return it to Him, and when they do not, they are stealing from God (Mal. 3:8–10).

When most people are behind financially and not making ends meet, giving ten percent of their already troubled income to God seems counterproductive. That is, unless they are like Joe and April, who believe in the goodness of God. Because they understand what the Bible teaches about the goodness of Jesus as their provider, going to the church website and making a payment with ten percent of their income becomes the first payment Joe and April want to make each month.

Joe and April discovered joy in the promise of God, which says, "'Bring the whole tithe into the storehouse, that there may be food in my house. Test me in this,' says the LORD Almighty, 'and see if I will not throw open the floodgates of heaven and pour out so much blessing that there will not be room enough to store it'" (Mal. 3:10).

With the third example in the previous chapter, I gave a hypothetical story about a tragedy, someone who was diagnosed with stage four cancer. What might the Word of God have to say about Jesus' goodness in that situation? As this person looks for the solution in passages of the Bible that involve God healing people, comparing and combining what passages from Matthew, Mark, Luke, and John reveal about people being healed from desperate health issues, he or she can understand that miracles do happen. Yet there is more to understand with the full picture about miracles from God. Jesus' goodness goes far beyond healing cancer.

Jesus will completely heal everyone who embraces a real relationship with Him. The Bible tells us, "Brothers and sisters, we do not want you to be uninformed about those who sleep in death, so that you do not grieve like the rest of mankind, who have no hope. For we believe that Jesus died and rose again, and so we believe that God will bring with Jesus those who have fallen asleep in him. According to the Lord's word, we tell you that we who are still alive, who are left until the coming of the Lord, will certainly not precede those who have fallen asleep. For the Lord himself will come down from heaven, with a loud command, with the voice of the archangel and with the trumpet call of God, and the dead in Christ will rise first. After that, we who are still alive and are left will be caught up together with them in the clouds to meet the Lord in the air. And so we will be with the Lord forever. Therefore encourage one another with these words" (1 Thess. 4:13–18). The problem in this passage is His followers not having hope about seeing fellow followers again. The solution is that, just as Jesus died and rose again in a resurrection, we can be confident that His followers who have died will rise again in a resurrection when He returns.

This means that everyone who takes the time to get to know Jesus, living as a follower, will be healed! It is just a matter of when. When Jesus returns, those who have died are resurrected, and those who are alive will be changed "in a flash, in the twinkling of an eye, at the last trumpet" (1 Cor. 15:52). Then, all the redeemed will be completely healed and live with Jesus in His heavenly kingdom forever and ever—no more cancer, no more diseases, pain, or sickness.

As you understand the solution to the problem and then compare and combine passages in the Bible, Bible topics become clear as you see how they reflect God's goodness. As you apply the solutions you learn in His Word to the issues you face, you will discover more about how faith (asking Him to help you trust in Him), God's goodness (His gifts), and believing (choosing to follow His answers) all help us in our relationship with Jesus. Understanding these basic elements in our relationship with Jesus leads to a growing relationship with Him.

To flourish in our relationship with Jesus, we need to get answers to our questions. Not answers that tell us what to do or excuse us from cooperating with Him, but answers that reveal His goodness.

Review: Discover the Power of Goodness and Find Your Answers

This simple reality exists: the life you live today reflects the answers you believe to the deepest questions in your soul. So the most important question becomes, where do you get your answers?

The problem we have with understanding the answers Jesus gives to our deepest questions comes from misunderstanding His priority in our lives. Jesus' priority is for us to get to know Him. Yet many people think that His role in our lives is to make us happy by doing the things we ask of Him. That perspective can become more entrenched in our thinking if we believe that the more faith we have the more He will do the things we ask Him. That is a false faith that leads to confusion and discouragement. With this false view of faith, when things go wrong (not the way we would like them to go) we can think of it as punishment. We imagine that Jesus is upset with us and punishing us by either not

> *Jesus' priority is for us to get to know Him. Yet many people think that His role in our lives is to make us happy by doing the things we ask of Him.*

doing what we ask or by bringing trouble into our lives because we did not have enough faith.

In order to embrace the answers Jesus seeks to give to our deepest questions, we need to understand how happiness that would come from fixing every challenge and making all of our dreams and wishes come true is not His priority, and, in reality, would not make us happy. Our happiness, joy, peace, and prosperity grow from the answers and opportunities He provides. So, to embrace His leading, we need to keep learning about His goodness. If we follow Jesus because we think that He will make us happy by making our wishes and dreams come true, we are following Him for the wrong reasons. The happiness and joy Jesus provides comes from getting to know Him, not from our false expectation that He should right every wrong and fix every problem.

Yes, Jesus does delight in helping us with the challenges we face. He walks with us through the troubles we encounter, no matter if they were from a mistake we made or not. Yet to understand the kind of help He provides we need to ask Him to help us understand His perspective. For example, sometimes His not answering a prayer in the way we believe it should be answered is the greatest blessing we can receive. As we learn more about His goodness, we can understand more about the options He seeks to provide that bring real help.

This world is not our home; we are pilgrims waiting for His heavenly kingdom. Jesus will be able to welcome us into His eternal kingdom if we allow Him to help us understand, experience, welcome, and embrace His way of thinking over our self-centered way of thinking. Jesus can give us new desires that reflect His way of thinking. Every person can discover the power of our Creator's goodness. Unfortunately, our self-focus comes installed at birth and does not go away, even with the new desires He provides. In fact, our self-focus and the new desires He provides create tension in our lives. Tension between choosing His goodness or our selfishness with every issue, conflict, and challenge we face.

We can resolve the tension, and enjoy making choices based on His goodness as we ask for and receive His help to trust in Him (faith). We can't understand His goodness without His help. If we make a choice based on our self-centered way of thinking, He gives us the opportunity to learn from our mistake. As we admit our mistake, He provides the healing of forgiveness. Then, even our mistakes become opportunities to learn more about His goodness.

When we misunderstand faith, we can set ourselves up for disappointment and even a dysfunctional relationship with Jesus in which we fail to understand real goodness. Consider these following questions and answers about faith.

> *Does faith influence how much Jesus can do for us in our lives? Yes.*
>
> *Does faith enable us to make choices that honor Jesus without His help? No.*
>
> *Does faith lead us to earn merit with God? No.*
>
> *Does faith lead us to know what we believe? Yes.*
>
> *Does faith mean we do not understand how God leads us and we will trust in Him anyway? No.*
>
> *Does faith mean we will always know how Jesus will resolve our issues, conflicts, or challenges in advance? No.*
>
> *Does faith mean that, if I just do not doubt, then God will give me what I want or what He wants? No.*

Does faith mean that Jesus helps me with my doubts as I get answers to my questions? Yes.

Does faith help us gain confidence in following Jesus? Yes.

Does faith mean we can get answers to our questions? Yes.

Does faith mean He will answer questions by helping us learn more about His goodness? Yes.

Does faith help us learn more about His love? Yes.

Does faith help us embrace the answers God provides, instead of the answers we think we need? Yes.

Does faith mean we understand that God will help us in His way and in His time with the answers He knows we need? Yes.

Does faith mean that, if we become convinced of God's will regarding an issue, we can manipulate people and tell half-truths so that God's will is done? No.

Does faith lead me to embrace Jesus' plan for my life without believing in His goodness? No.

Does faith mean that God leads us to understand His will as we ask for His help with our choices? Yes.

Does living a faithful life mean that Jesus makes our happiness His priority by dissolving every problem? No.

Does a life of faith mean, as we ask for His help to trust in Him, that sometimes, in His way and in His time, He will intervene in our lives to help us in ways we could have never imagined? Yes.

Does the happiness and joy that comes from knowing Jesus exceed the happiness that could come from having every problem we face resolved by Jesus as <u>we think</u> it should be resolved? Yes.

Does faith mean that Jesus will help me understand and apply His love and goodness to my life? Yes.

Does faith mean we will learn more and more about His love and goodness so that one day we will not even need His help with the choices we make? No.

Does faith create a relationship with Jesus in which we learn how to understand and apply His gifts to our lives instead of expecting Him to tell us what to do like a robot? Yes.

Faith: Asking Jesus for Help to Trust in Him

If we have faith, does it mean that God will shield us from disappointments, misfortune, unfair circumstances, prejudice, cruelty, cancer, disease, tragedies, or conflicts? If we believe that our faith will shield us from all these things then, when things go wrong, we will blame God. We will come to believe that God is not doing His part to help us, and we can even begin to think that God is against us. So what is faith?

Faith is trust. Faith is asking Jesus for help to trust Him. We experience faith as a relationship in which we ask for and receive Jesus' help to trust in Him in all that we will encounter in this life. We can learn to trust Him as we welcome the work of the Holy Spirit to create His goodness in our hearts and minds. As we welcome the gifts Jesus provides, we can understand the difference between His love and our self-centered way of thinking. Then we can embrace His answers to our questions, making choices that honor Him as we receive the strength we need to follow through on the choice He led us to make.

Faith allows a relationship with Jesus to flourish. A relationship that is based on a routine of getting answers to the deepest questions in our souls as He answers us with

His goodness. Over time, as understanding and confidence in His goodness grow, we can more easily choose to follow the answers He provides. Accepting the answers He provides is contingent on receiving His help to trust in Him, which then allows us to understand and experience more and more of His goodness.

Faith Bible Verses.

Proverbs 3:5,6; Hebrews 11:1–6; James 1:1–5; Psalm 37:3–7; Psalm 44:6–8; Psalm 62:5–8; Psalm 119:103–105; Matthew 6:22–24; Matthew 11:28–30; John 3:16–21; John 8:12; John 12:46; 1 John 1:5–10; Matthew 16:5–12; Romans 3:20–24; Galatians 3:9–14; 2 Timothy 4:7,8

Goodness: How Jesus Answers

How will Jesus answer our questions in a way that helps us trust in Him? Jesus will answer our questions the only way He can, with His goodness. Jesus is always good, and it is His goodness that defines Him. That means, as we journey with Him, we must be willing to learn about His goodness.

Our focus needs to be on getting to know Him better and applying His goodness to our lives, not on trying to do the right thing or just seeking relief from our difficulties. Often His answers do not fix our problems or instantly resolve our issues, but rather they give us insights into His goodness that help us know Him better and understand ourselves more. As we seek to get to know Him better, to understand and apply His goodness to our lives, we can embrace the answers He provides.

> *Jesus is always good, and it is His goodness that defines Him.*

Three ways to ask Jesus to help you understand His goodness so you can understand His answers.

First, ask Jesus to help you trust that He always wants the best option for you. Jesus is always good. However, people are not. Jesus is always good, and He is all-powerful, but He will not force people to follow His way of thinking. That means the unfair, prejudiced, self-centered, evil things that happen to you do not come from Him. While Jesus does not force people to follow His way, at times He does intervene on your behalf with the issues, challenges, and situations you face. Jesus always wants the best option for you, but people can interfere with His plans and, even with the best option, you might have to endure some suffering.

Second, ask Jesus to help you by creating the gifts of His goodness in your heart. Jesus is our all-powerful Creator; He can create goodness in your heart and mind. He can give you peace, when you do not have peace, joy when you have no joy, or hope when you feel hopeless. He can create goodness in your heart just as He created the sun, stars, trees, rocks, animals, and humans. The goodness He places in your heart will defuse the frustration, anxiety, or worry, and you will have an opportunity to understand His answer to your question. Verses for further study: Ezekiel 11:19; Psalm 51:10; John 14:27; 2 Corinthians 5:17; Titus 3:5; Hebrews 10:16

Third, ask Him to help you remember what He has taught you about His goodness in the past. Jesus will bring to your mind things He has taught you about His love and goodness in His Word. He will help you remember experiences that reveal how He has provided His forgiveness, grace, healing, hope, and wisdom, as described in the Bible. He can bring to your mind experiences you have had in the past or the experiences of others that will give you insights. Take time to write a few things down about His goodness that come to your mind. Such as *I know Jesus gives me the healing of forgiveness, I know Jesus gives me wisdom*, and *I know Jesus will provide for my future.* Verses for further study: Isaiah 49:15–16; Psalm 143:5; John 14:26; Psalm 103:2; Psalm 119:11; Hebrews 4:12

Bible Verses that Reveal the Goodness of God

Romans 2:4; Galatians 5:22; 2 Peter 1:3,4; Exodus 34:6; Psalm 145:9; Mark 10:18; James 1:17; Matthew 7:11; Psalm 107:8,9; Psalm 69:16; Psalm 107;1; Jeremiah 29:11; Romans 5:8; Romans 8:28; Jeremiah 29:11; Psalm 32:8; Isaiah 40:31;1 Corinthians 2:9; Psalm 56:8

Believe: Choosing to Follow the Answers Jesus Provides

Jesus provides insights. When Jesus provides insights about how to apply His goodness to your issues, conflicts, and challenges, you can choose to follow His answer. To believe means to choose, to make a commitment to the answers He provides. Then you need to ask for His help to follow through with the commitment you have made.

Jesus will help you. He will help you apply what He has taught you about His goodness in His Word to the issue, conflict, or challenge you ask Him about. That means you may not get a direct answer to your question. You may get an answer that reveals how His goodness applies to your question. In this way, you get to know Jesus better as you embrace the process of applying His goodness to your life. You will be amazed at the wonderful insights Jesus will give you as you apply His love, His goodness, to your life. A next step for you to take will become clear as you understand how His goodness answers your question.

Believe Bible Verses

Matthew 16:24; John 8:12; Matthew 7:21–23; 1 John 2:3–4; John 10:27; John 15:14; John 12:26; John 15:5–8; Matthew 6:33; John 3:16–20; John 8:31

The Agreement

Discovering the power of God's goodness so you can embrace His answers is based on the agreement Jesus designed for our salvation. The Bible calls it the *Everlasting Covenant*. As with all covenants or agreements, each party in the agreement has a part. Our part of the agreement is to believe by faith. To believe by faith means we ask for Jesus help to trust in Him with the choices we make.

God's part of the agreement is to provide the gifts we need to have a relationship in which we can trust in Him. As we ask for Jesus' help, He will provide gifts (assurance, love, joy, peace, patience, kindness, goodness, gentleness, faithfulness, self-control, wisdom, courage, discernment, etc.) that enable us trust in Him. His gifts will help us to understand His goodness as revealed in His Word and the answers He seeks to provide to our questions. These gifts help us to understand the difference between His way of thinking and our way of thinking.

It is important to realize that the Bible defines faith as trust and believing as our choice. To trust is a state of mind, while believing is an action word.

As we believe by faith (ask Him for help to trust in Him with the choices we make), He provides the gifts we need to trust in and understand His way of thinking. As we choose to accept (believe) His gifts, He enables us to understand how His solutions to the problems presented in Bible passages help us understand His answers to our questions. The solutions we discover in His Word will also help us to understand more about His gifts and how they work in our lives.

This means that, when we ask for Jesus' help to trust in Him, He provides the gifts we need to experience His goodness, understand His solutions in His Word, and then embrace His answers to our deepest questions. The gifts He creates in our hearts and minds, the solutions He provides in His Word, and the answers He provides to our questions all work in unity together to help us with the choices we make in life. The graphic below illustrates how faith, gifts, and belief (the agreement) work together to help us understand His solutions and His answers. For more information about *the agreement,* read the book *You Are a Child of the King and He Has an Inheritance for You* by Keith Trumbo. This book is available at www.TEACHServices.com and www.Amazon.com.

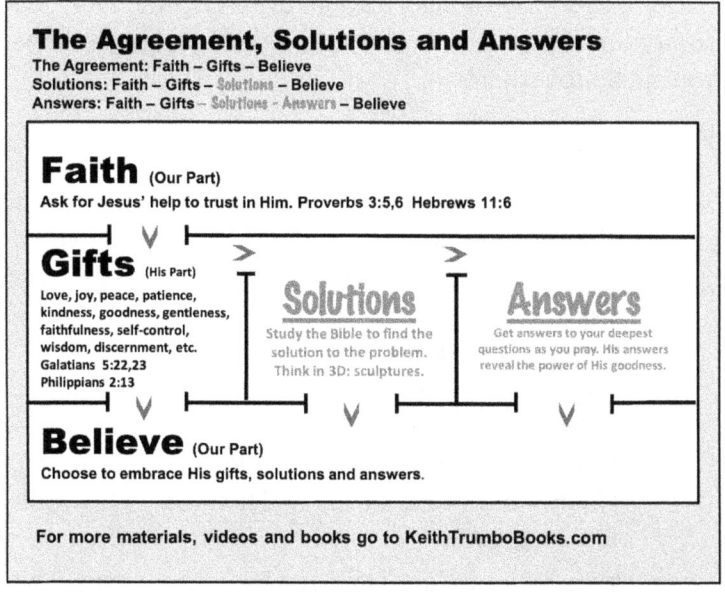

Have you understood what it means to believe by faith? Do you embrace His goodness that includes the healing of forgiveness each day? If you have not, you can experience the power of Jesus' love in a way you have not before.

Just try it!, Ask Jesus for His help to trust in Him, then welcome the precious gifts He seeks to give you each day that will help you understand the difference between His way of thinking and your self-centered way of thinking.

Take the Ten-day Challenge

You can get real answers to the deepest questions in your heart. Just try relating to Jesus as described in the outline below. You will be surprised and amazed at how you can get answers to your questions from Jesus. Try it for ten days. It does not have to be ten consecutive days. Maybe you could try it for ten days over the span of 18 days.

To take the ten-day challenge, you will need a special place to keep your notes. You can use a document on your computer, a paper notebook, journal, or just some paper you staple together.

Follow this outline.

1. Ask Jesus for His help to trust in Him with the choices you face. Put the issue, challenge, or situation you face into a question to ask Jesus. Take the time to write down your question. Most people ask either "why" questions or "how" questions. It's good to start by getting an answer to "why" first. Then with a clear understanding of "why," you can begin to ask "how." For example, "Why can't I lose weight?" Then ask, "How can I lose weight?"

2. Let Jesus know why you are asking Him this question.

3. Ask Jesus for His help to understand His answer in the three ways listed below:

    a. "Please help me trust that you will guide me to understand the best option, based on Your goodness, even though people can interfere with your plans and the best option might include suffering."
    b. "Please create the gifts of Your goodness; your love, joy, peace, patience, kindness, goodness, gentleness, faithfulness, self-control, wisdom, and discernment in my heart right now."
    c. "Please help me remember the solutions you have taught me in your Word and how what I have learned applies to my question."

4. As Jesus helps you trust in Him by creating His goodness in your heart and mind, and helps you to remember the solutions He has revealed to you in His Word, ask Him to help you listen to His goodness in your heart and mind to gain insights about your question. Write down any thoughts that come to your mind about the question you asked. He will give you insights from the perspective of His goodness. He may not give you a direct answer, so be ready for the answer He seeks to provide that gives you insights into His goodness and your motives and desires. Remember, a real relationship with Jesus that is based on biblical faith means we understand that His first priority is not to make us happy by answering all of our requests in the way we think He should. His first priority is to help us understand, experience, and accept His goodness as the way to approach our choices in life.

5. As you write down the answers or insights Jesus provides, let Him know that you choose to follow

the answer He has provided. Remember, you will need to ask for His help to keep the commitment you are making to follow His answer.

You can discover the power of God's goodness and get real answers to the deepest questions in your heart. Jesus delights in answering your questions. He enjoys helping you learn more about His way of thinking. Remember that He will talk to you in the language of love, which is a language you do not naturally understand, so you must have His help to understand His goodness.

May God richly bless you as you seek to embrace His goodness with the choices you make!

TEACH Services, Inc.
P U B L I S H I N G

We invite you to view the complete
selection of titles we publish at:
www.TEACHServices.com

We encourage you to write us
with your thoughts about this,
or any other book we publish at:
info@TEACHServices.com

TEACH Services' titles may be purchased in
bulk quantities for educational, fund-raising,
business, or promotional use.
bulksales@TEACHServices.com

Finally, if you are interested in seeing
your own book in print, please contact us at:
publishing@TEACHServices.com

We are happy to review your manuscript at no charge.

www.ingramcontent.com/pod-product-compliance
Lightning Source LLC
Chambersburg PA
CBHW070544170426
43200CB00011B/2547